THE EDUCATION

OF A

DIPLOMAT

By HUGH WILSON

with an Introduction by

CLAUDE G. BOWERS

LONDON, NEW YORK, TORONTO

LONGMANS, GREEN AND CO.

1938

LONGMANS, GREEN AND CO.
114 FIFTH AVENUE, NEW YORK
221 EAST 20TH STREET, CHICAGO
88 TREMONT STREET, BOSTON

LONGMANS, GREEN AND CO. LTD.
39 PATERNOSTER ROW, LONDON, E.C. 4
CHITTARANJAN AVENUE, CALCUTTA
53 NICOL ROAD, BOMBAY
36A MOUNT ROAD, MADRAS

LONGMANS, GREEN AND CO.
215 VICTORIA STREET, TORONTO

WILSON
THE EDUCATION OF A DIPLOMAT

COPYRIGHT · 1938
BY HUGH WILSON

FIRST EDITION

PRINTED IN THE UNITED STATES OF AMERICA

THE EDUCATION OF A DIPLOMAT

To
KATE

INTRODUCTION

In 1911 Hugh Wilson entered the Foreign Service of the United States as the private secretary of the Minister to Lisbon. Thence he went to Guatemala, and that fascinating country made an indelible impression on his imagination which is reflected in some of the most charming pages of this book. After a period in the Embassy at Buenos Aires, he was transferred to Europe and, from the Embassy in Berlin, he was privileged to observe at close quarters the reactions of a great nation to the tremendous struggle in which it faced a large part of a hostile world in arms. It was from this point of vantage that he saw the United States drawn into the vortex; and when, with Gerard and the staff of the Embassy, he crossed the frontier on the breaking of diplomatic relations, he saw grim history in the making. After a brief assignment in Vienna, with which we were hastening to a rupture, he was sent to the Legation in Switzerland, perhaps the best international observation post in the world, for the remainder of the war.

After the conclusion of the peace he was sent back to Berlin and to Tokyo, and such was the confidence he had inspired in his superiors in the State Department that he was called upon to play a part in the development of our Foreign Service in Washington and to serve on numerous international commissions. For ten years he was the American Minister in Switzerland, where, as observer and reporter of the plays on the checkerboard of international politics, he has rendered an invaluable service to the country, little known to the general

vii

public, but appreciated by those charged with the direction of our foreign affairs.

It is because his service has been distinguished that recently he was summoned home to serve as Assistant Secretary of State.

In this unpretentious book he has set down memories and impressions covering the first phase of his diplomatic career, beginning with his novice days in Lisbon and ending with the entry of the United States into the Great War. So charmingly and entertainingly has he done so that it is to be hoped he may continue these reminiscences whenever, in his judgment, it may be done with professional propriety.

The Foreign Service men of other nations, particularly those of Britain and France, have produced a literature of delightful and illuminating memoirs. But few non-professional American diplomats have written memoirs or published letters. The letters of Page, the memoirs of Whitlock, the two books of Gerard instantly suggest themselves; and in his sprightly *Castilian Days* John Hay have given us a contribution of another kind. But at the moment I do not recall that any of our Foreign Service men of career have set down their observations and impressions on the printed page with the exception of Hugh Gibson, who dealt largely with abnormal times and problems.

Mr. Wilson, therefore, may create a precedent to be followed by others in the Foreign Service who well may profit by this accomplished diplomat's perfect tact, fine sense of selection, and ready realization of what is best left unsaid.

A crisis involving the peace of the world could scarcely cause more distress and perturbation in the State Department than the suggestion that all the career men were about to become articulate on paper. But happily there is no possibility of an indiscriminate revelation of state secrets. In the case of the younger men some seasoning years must pass before their own impressions can become definite and fixed ; and in the case of the seasoned, there is little danger of indiscretions.

And now that we of America are becoming conscious of the outside world, and of its reactions on our national life, there should be a keener appreciation of the work of our Foreign Service and a more intelligent understanding of the public servants who bear the burden in the field. When we finally emerge from our traditional provincialism, it will seem incredible that as late as our own day we spent almost as much on our Bureau of Indian Affairs as on the Foreign Service which is charged with the defense of American lives and the protection of billions in property, and is entrusted with the task of cultivating friendly relations, and with the preservation of peace. Surely the time has come to erase from the public mind some of the prejudices against this conscientious and zealous corps of state servants.

The Foreign Service diplomat has self-effacement imposed upon him. A British Minister of Foreign Affairs once expressed the fate of these inconspicuous but essential workers in a few words — 'always present and never seen.' When criticized unjustly, they cannot defend themselves before the public ; and no matter how brilliant their success, they cannot toot their own horn.

The popular notion of the career men of the diplomatic service is ridiculously unfair. According to this concept these men live merely to toy with tea-cups and cocktail glasses, to stuff on terrapin and caviar, to play golf by day and bridge by night, and to wear spats and carry slender canes. Yet constantly and laboriously, though inconspicuously, they serve the interest of the country, smoothe the threatening wrinkles of international misunderstandings, conciliate differences, cultivate friendships, and guard the interests of their countrymen in foreign lands.

In periods of outer serenity all this is accepted without recognition or appreciation. But when troubles come, when property is imperiled and lives endangered, the most flippant of the scoffers are the first to find their way to the embassies, legations, and consulates to throw themselves on the protection of these men of the Foreign Service — and never in vain. For a moment the diplomat of career may be acclaimed, but when the troubles pass and the drama fades, and he resumes the even tenor of his way, his services are apt to be forgotten.

It is not generally realized that there has been a constant improvement in the personnel of our Foreign Service since its organization on a professional non-political basis during Mr. Root's tenure in the State Department. In the early days of the Republic, before we had a professional diplomacy, we were fortunate in finding our envoys among the foremost statesmen of the country. The Adamses, Jefferson, Monroe, and Pinckney could have challenged comparison with the best of their contemporaries. But in time there was a marked deterioration in the political appointments, and the high standard of the first days of the Republic was not maintained. More and more, under the new dispensation, the heads of missions are being found among the diplomats of career. No one has taken a longer step in this direction than President Roosevelt.

I am sure such books as this may aid in bringing a fairer popular appraisement of the men who represent us beyond our frontiers.   But there is another reason why they should be welcomed.   In these days when literary adventurers make hurried journeys into foreign lands to emerge with fat volumes, written ex cathedra, and filled with misinformation, it is refreshing to come across the observations of men who have sojourned long enough to have a bowing acquaintance with the country.   And no one is better qualified to make such observations than the members of the Foreign Service.

It is not the possession of their real knowledge which gives the charm to diplomatic memoirs.   The historian of today wishing to recapture the atmosphere of other times, and to recreate the flesh and blood likeness of the actors of another age, knows that there is no better source of material than the confidential despatches of diplomats to their masters.

And the personal contacts of the diplomat are always interesting.   One comes into friendly, and sometimes intimate, contact with personalities that are making history.   The more sensitive and penetrating realize that they are permitted to look upon the stage setting of historic events from the wings.   They see the scene shifters at their work, the subterfuges to deceive the eye of the audience in front, the smudge upon the scenery, the patches on the curtain.   The great audience in front sees the effect desired, but only he who is in the wings knows how it has been managed.

Mr. Wilson's pages have the simplicity of sincerity, the charm of mellow memories, and the pleasant philosophy of a refreshing toleration.   Few will read the chapters on Guatemala without a desire to seek these entrancing scenes, and no one will lay the book aside without a better understanding of the spirit and the character of the keen and tactful men of our Foreign Service whose achievements are mostly buried in the archives, and who, 'while always present, are never seen.'

CLAUDE G. BOWERS

PREFACE

The first chapter of my diplomatic experience was ended when the United States went to war. All Americans of my generation feel, I think, that our entry into the war put a definite end to the life they had known before. Indeed I have often heard the observation from the lips of friends of my age that our lives have been divided into three portions : before the war, during the war, and after the war. Curiously enough they have often added that in retrospect the three portions seem of almost equal duration. In my case, certainly, the beginning of a new period was evident even at the time. I became deeply and immediately engrossed in political work and could express my views and struggle for them in the field of American policy. Up to this point I had been a part of the machine in the Embassies, and my participation in the political field had been vicarious. Then it became direct.

This change from preparation to practice, from youth to maturity, represented a change, as well, in my attitude toward the Foreign Service. In my mind it ceased to be the temporary enjoyable means of passing a few years. I no longer considered it a pleasant interval only. The work had become something so engrossing that I hoped to devote my life to it. It had ceased to be a diversion, it had become a profession which made my interests coincide with my work. History, languages, habits and manner of thought of peoples, their economic, sociological and financial problems, all fell within the orbit of this profession. Study of all these interested me and at the same time increased my usefulness for the work I was doing. The profession of the Foreign Service necessitates study, continuous study, the succession of new posts brings rapidly changing problems. New civilizations must be understood in order that reports can be adequate and advice as to our government's policy useful. I found that it was a profession which called for the best I had in me, and in which, at our entry into the war, I began to feel myself competent.

The disadvantages of diplomatic life are obvious. Your years are spent in alien groups in which you have no real roots. You never become an integral part of any community with its obligations and compensations in the close contact with life-long friends. Your fate is decided in what may seem to you an arbitrary manner, dependent upon accident or personal relationship. You may never be given the particular work in which you are most deeply interested and in which you feel yourself most competent. Monetary rewards are modest, the opportunity for saving non-existent. In the youthful American service there is always the probability of the continued appointment of political men to the highest posts. In our service, furthermore, the act of a diplomatic officer is rarely of such vital importance to his nation as, for instance, that of the diplomat of Great Britain or France. Nations of the continent are continually pursuing definite policies that they regard as of vital importance, that may indeed preserve the peace of the continent against the menace of war. We are so blessed by geography that our foreign policy seldom becomes of first importance in the opinion of the people of the United States.

But there are compensations in the life, and these are real and enduring. There is a satisfaction in Government service, a sense of duty accomplished, which is missed profoundly by those who withdraw from the Service to enter other tasks. There is the satisfaction of continuous study, and study directly applicable to the work in hand.   Further, the Foreign Service Officer has access to the most interesting minds and personalities in all nations where he resides.   Whether he maintains relations with them or not depends upon his own resources and capabilities.   At least he has access to them.   He will find his satisfaction in the day-by-day task, in the people of interest whom he encounters, in places, scenes, glimpses of unexpected beauty, and in the chance which only comes rarely, of influencing his own government's policy.   Such must be his compensation ; he must not count too much on finding his satisfaction in future recognition.

For this profession as in few others the impulse and desire to do the thing must be overwhelming, and if any man enters the service regarding it as something less than a vocation, he will lead an unhappy and disillusioned existence.

HUGH WILSON

Berne, Switzerland
June 1937

CHAPTER I

One January evening in 1912 I sat with my brother and his family in his house in Evanston. The door-bell rang and a telegram was handed me by which the Secretary of State informed me that I had been appointed Secretary of Legation to Guatemala. A clamor at once broke out in the family for knowledge of that remote land, so I pulled down the Encyclopedia and read aloud somewhat as follows : 'Guatemala — the most populous and the second largest country of Central America ; population approximately 3,000,000, mostly Indian ; principal industry, coffee growing ; capital Guatemala City ; form of government — democratic constitution, but present President, Manuel Estrada Cabrera, has been in office fourteen years and exercises dictatorial power.'

Two years before, my mother had died. Thus I had no further obligation to remain at home, the family house was to be sold, and I inherited an income sufficient to enable me to follow my inclinations. I had been three years in business and, while I was probably as well equipped for that type of life as the majority of young Americans with a university degree, I rather imagine I was more unhappy than the majority during the years of my business experience.

My real life was outside my office, in my books, in my friends, in my amusements. The coincidence of intellectual taste with work in hand is indispensable to success. The divergence between my tastes and my business was becoming daily more plain to me. Aside from a certain knowledge of business procedure which has stood me in good stead, the only business experience that I cherish is the fact that for three years and more I reached my office every morning at eight o'clock, and this from a distance of twelve miles. Of that I am proud, somewhat as an old mountain climber thinks back on the peaks he has scaled in his youth.

Something seemed wrong with a world in which life was regulated by rigid hours. I could already understand hard work and the pleasure in it. The numerous periods of my life of intense activity have been the most satisfactory. Never subsequently, however, have I been obliged to spend hours in an office when my work was finished, never since have I had to devote myself to a task which had no possible relation to matters of real interest to me. The practice of the professions doubtless brings about that coincidence of taste with labor which diplomacy gives so generously, but to me, at least, mercantile life gave not a pretense of it.

If I am to make clear the spirit in which I began to make plans for the diplomatic service, I must try to recapture the state of mind of a great many young people of the United States in the decade before the war. I have tried to picture this to my son and I realize the enormous difficulty of making that state of mind real to those who did not live through it. Indeed it is difficult enough for us who were young in those years to thrust ourselves back and recapture the thoughts that were ours before the Great War. We were born in the Victorian era. When we reached manhood the Franco-Prussian War was long past, tales of the Civil War bored us to tears, and the Russo-Japanese and the Boer Wars were in such remote parts of the world as to be interesting only as episodes of history. Even the Spanish War was too easy and romantic — it inspired visions of world power but not of cataclysm. Change in the world was inconceivable; change in our social relations might come, but it would not be on a scale to shake our fundamental institutions. War between civilized Western Powers was an absurdity — 'it would cost too much'; 'the international bankers would never permit it'; 'the Socialist parties in Europe would call a general strike.' The world had become more or less democratic and surely, we argued, this trend toward democracy would become ever stronger, and peaceful democracies all over the world would avoid war. Investment had the same element of immutability — we bought bonds and stocks to hold for a score of years or a lifetime. My family in unquestioning faith bought Pullman and Illinois Central and Chicago bank stock whenever there was cash for investment. These securities had treated our fathers well; surely they would do the same for us. What we lacked wholly was historical perspective. To us the Victorian era of stability was normal. We needed a lifetime to realize, and some of us have not yet realized, that the Victorian era was an historical phenomenon, so unusual that it will be cited with the age of Augustus as one of the two great periods of peace and security in the history of western civilization. We lived in the illusion of immutability, but we had unquestioning faith in the illusion.

This assumption of the unchanging nature of our institutions was tempered by, and to some extent gave rise to, a feeling that the 'American way' of our fathers was not one which of necessity we had to follow. Our fathers had moved west in the great migrations. They had been builders. They had had to struggle through their youth to achieve that stability which we young men assumed was normal. We found it difficult to understand the grimness with which they faced life. We had less sympathy with the continued pursuit of the amassing of fortunes. We found it hard to accept the type of successful man of affairs as the standard for our emulation. Ease and a measure of education had encouraged us to believe that life should have a wider scope than business alone could offer.

So when I broached to my father's friends my idea of entering the diplomatic service I found that a chasm separated the two generations. Without the encouragement of my brother Oliver I doubt if I would have carried through my intention. Oliver was eight years older than I, and from the time of my father's death, when I was fifteen, had done his best, and a very good best, to give me that advice and example of which father's death deprived me. Oliver's personality was one of the most lovable I have known. Gay and buoyant, he was unselfish to a degree that became selflessness. In appearance he had no relation to his brothers and sisters, his hair and complexion were like those of an Indian, his hands were sensitive and beautifully shaped like an artist's. He was devoted to his family, and his friends could do no wrong. He worked at high intensity, but he would play with equal enthusiasm. On a vacation trip he was the most joyous of companions, and on the golf course or the tennis court his whole-hearted absorption and good humor made him a beloved companion. As I said, in my thoughts of the diplomatic service he not only encouraged me but he did better : he accompanied me to Florida to visit my uncle, the President of our corporation and the only one of his generation in our family still alive at that time.

My uncle was a type which is rapidly disappearing in the United States. An officer in the Civil War, he married immediately thereafter and entered the business of his older brother. He saw objects, acts, and motives as black and white only. His integrity was unimpeachable. He was a wise administrator. The business was run with a degree of conservatism which made it impregnable as long as it was under his control. He was a church-goer of clock-like regularity ; his tall black-clad figure used to stride up our front stairs punctually at 10:20 on Sunday mornings to accompany my mother to church with such of the children as could be induced to join in the procession. He reached his business at eight sharp, took the elevator to the tenth floor, walked rapidly around it, descended one flight, made a circuit there, and so on down to his office on the ground floor. Those of us working on the second floor could count on about twelve minutes' grace. He was generous in charity and works of education, parsimonious to a degree in his personal life. I never saw a scratch pad on his desk ; he said that the envelopes of incoming letters furnished all the paper he needed for calculations. He was tall and grim and lonely. In my youthful mind I admired him intensely, occasionally he interested me deeply, but I never could escape a certain exasperation that his success and uprightness had left him so aloof and so utterly incapable of the ordinary pleasures in which my father, his younger brother, rejoiced to the day of his death. Perhaps the best example of his character was the disposition of his property. With a number of relatives in various parts of the United States badly in need of financial assistance, he left practically all of his considerable fortune to

Northwestern University, of which he was not even a graduate.   Years later, when I was appointed Minister to Switzerland, I received a letter from him offering his congratulations
and good wishes.   I thanked him, and that was the only time
that the subject of my profession was reopened between us.
I like to believe from his letter that as the years went on he
became more reconciled to the career I had chosen.   Our interview in Florida was painful.   He did not hide his disap-
proval of my plans and made it clear to me that in adhering to
them he considered that I would be remiss in my duty.

Without exception, my father's friends also warned me
against the step I was taking.   They declared with reason that
diplomacy in the United States was the football of politics;
that there was no money in it and usually ended by saying
that 'frivolous society in Europe was no place for a young
American.'   They had no belief whatever in the prospects of
the youthful services for diplomats and consuls.   They were
sure the services would be wrecked by succeeding Presidents.

As a matter of fact, with most of their attacks I was in complete agreement.   There was no money in it, certainly, but I
thought I had enough for comfort; and though I had seen the
panic of 1907, that of 1929 was inconceivable.   It was the
plaything of politics, yes: the knowledge of the service they
gave me added to what I already knew of the extent of the
spoils system in its administration.   The American service
abroad has shown numerous examples of outstanding personalities, Franklin, Jefferson, Monroe and others, but they
were the exceptions.   The American public knows of them
and is rightly proud of them.   They know little or nothing of
the political hacks sent to the great majority of posts.   They

do not realize that for years, and especially after the Civil War, America was represented abroad largely by the failures at home, by the relatives and friends of those in authority who had been unable to make a living for themselves or whose absence gave their families a momentary relief. I had gone around the world in 1906 and had seen some of our representatives and had shared the indignation they provoked among American travellers. At that time I had not yet heard of the classic example, the broken-down livery-stable keeper whom President Grant nominated for a diplomatic post. This is not the place to talk of what has been done in thirty years to improve the situation; I will do so later. I knew these things, and I learned more, but I still felt that I could have an amusing and interesting existence for a few years and then get out and return to the stable and everlasting world that I had known.

Largely as a result of these conversations, I went into the service with my eyes opened. I expected nothing but the daily satisfaction of the life itself. I had no illusions. Thus the patient growth of the service idea has been all velvet, so to speak. The setbacks to the service and its slow development have disappointed many others, but they have never disappointed me because I expected much less when I entered and have been pleased by every sign of progress, however slow. But one thing I know — the service has given that satisfaction in every-day life, in the work of the moment, which my instinct told me I would find, and I would not exchange the years that have passed with anyone. I will go more into this subject later. Perhaps what I can tell of some of these years will do more to explain the satisfaction than any analysis could do.

The race of man has endured some millions of years, yet

every generation is convinced of the errors of the old men, of their stodgy methods and outworn conventions. My father told me of his departure from the farm and how he was accused of running away from his duty. I have told of my disputes as to leaving business and entering diplomacy. Youths of the generation of my son repeat until one says it first to take the wind out of their sails, 'The old men brought on the war. Why should we listen to them ?' It is safe to assume that the sons of *pithecanthropus erectus* left the cave in disgust to scratch on the rocks cartoons of the old man being chased by a mastodon. Even in Eastern civilizations with the cult of the old in life and of the ancestor in death, I wonder if the young men don't go through the forms with their tongues in their cheeks — they know so much better ! So in spite of the warning of my elders, I felt instinctively that the diplomatic service could give me something that I could find in no other task.

I knew one man in the diplomatic service, Arthur Orr. He was born in Evanston, as I was, and we had played together as children. My father's friends had reluctantly supplied me with letters to the Senators from Illinois, to the Secretary of State and other exalted gentlemen. They were not the ones I wanted to talk to. I wanted to talk to my contemporary, Arthur, and see what his few years of experience had meant to him. So I sent Arthur a telegram, proceeded to Washington and took him to dine at Harvey's. Before dinner was over my decision was fixed. Arthur was as disillusioned as a young man should be, but he said he was having a glorious time and only regretted that his rapidly enlarging family had increased his expenses to the point where he would have to get out. When I questioned him about the future of the service, 'You won't get anywhere,' said Arthur, 'but you will have a lot of fun going there.'

On the train going east I had run into Hugh Knox, Hootie, we called him at Yale. When he heard what I had in mind he took me into the drawing room to meet his father, Mr. Philander Knox, at that time Secretary of State. The son resembled the father to an almost comical degree. The Secretary was a short, round man, with a clean-shaven oval face, formidable nose and egg-shaped head. When he smiled the face was a mass of humorous wrinkles. One of the best lawyers in the United States, his humor was sardonic and devastating, and would break through the most serious moments. He had an air of enjoying his life that was appealing. I grew fond of him and relished his caustic observation of humanity, but I never felt entirely free from the fear that I might at any moment be the victim of one of his shafts, and sometimes I was.

Secretary Knox didn't think much of the diplomatic service, but invited me to stay at his house in Washington and see what the State Department looked like. He added, 'I'm glad you turned up ; now that we are three we can play poker.' He laid down the rules. Hootie and I were to have five dollars worth of chips ; as soon as the Secretary had got them from us the game was over. He got them. This lesson of what the expert could do to the novice at that game has kept me out of poker for the rest of my life.

I enjoyed staying at his house. The Secretary was a man of deceptive impression. He seemed lazy but was the only Secretary of State I have ever seen who had his desk clear and time to receive everybody. He loved a good story, and any member of the Department who acquired one rushed down to the Secretary's office to deliver it.   A certain risk was involved, if the Secretary had heard it before, he threw you out with contumely.   He rose every morning at 4:30 to 5 and got in an immense amount of work before breakfast.   So when he took his hat and stick and strolled out it was as a man of leisure, stopping to chat with acquaintances on the way, his funny little round face creased in smiles.   Mrs. Knox was a kindly hostess and a lovable woman, but quite deaf.   So she and the Secretary rarely went out to dinner and then only on the most official and unescapable invitations.

It was Huntington Wilson, First Assistant Secretary of State, who gave me my real advice as to how to prepare for the examinations.   His reputation was that of a bloodless machine, and his appearance accorded with his reputation, but no one could have been kinder.   When we were talking in his office the card of the Danish Minister was brought to him. He said to the messenger, 'Tell the Danish Minister that he must wait ; I have made an appointment for this time.'   I felt immensely important.   He advised me to stay away from the cramming school and go to the Ecole Libre des Sciences Politiques at Paris.   He made an argument that I have often used since to boys thinking of taking their examinations.   He said, 'It is relatively easy under our requirements to learn enough French or German to pass the examinations.   But the difference between such a knowledge of French and a real knowledge makes the difference between boredom and pleasure in diplomacy.   Wherever you go, men and women of intelligence, education, and charm will speak French and unless you are really at home in the tongue, your relations with such people will be tedious instead of being full of interest, as they should be.' It was the most useful item of advice that anyone gave me, and its truth is confirmed week after week and year after year when I see the relative isolation of diplomats of all countries if they are not at home in French.

I also called on Mr. Adee, at that time the only permanent officer in the Department. Adee had already become a tradition in the Department, but a tradition that was still full of vigor. He had served for a lifetime and had made himself indispensable to Secretaries of State of all shades of political opinion and of every sort of temperament. One has only to read the biographies of men like Root and Hay to realize the confidence that the Secretaries placed in Adee, to appreciate his forcefulness and the great influence he exerted on our foreign policy through more than two score years. To the general public he was obscure, but his very obscurity contrasted with his real significance renders him a fascinating study. His role has some of the reticence and significance of Holstein, in the German Foreign Office before the war, but none of the sinister influence of the latter. Adee represents my conception in American history of the great public servant.

When I called I saw a small man of sandy and dusty appearance seated at a desk so crowded with papers that he could barely see over them. The room itself was littered with books and dossiers on the chairs, on the floor, and bursting from the shelves.

He gave me his ear-trumpet to shout through, told me a couple of stories and made a few caustic remarks that deflated my ego. It's a pity that there was no Boswell to compile the philosophy of Mr. Adee through record of his conversation. He was a salty personality, a man of independent and original judgment. Washington was full of his remarks at that time, and I regret that I remember only one of the many. On the occasion of his 25th anniversary of service in the Department his friends got up a dinner for him. Several speeches were made to which Adee listened indulgently through his ear-trumpet. John Barrett, Director of the Pan-American Union, a speaker of thunderous phrases, took the floor. 'From the pine-clad hills of Maine to the flower-lit vales of California, from the mighty rivers of Oregon to the palmetto plains of Florida,' boomed Mr. Barrett. Adee folded his ear-trumpet, put it in his pocket and remarked to his neighbor, 'There are advantages in being deaf — you can break the connection.' Mr. Adee's record of long service in the Department has only been equalled, I imagine, by that of Mr. Wilbur Carr, who after forty odd years of service has just been appointed Minister to Prague.

Huntington Wilson's advice to go to Paris suited me admirably. I had been reading a good deal of French but it was the books of such writers as Poe and Leonard Merrick that really made me eager to spend some time there. Eighteenth-century France I had regarded as the finest flower of civilization, and though France of the twentieth century seemed to have lost some of its flavor, I was eager to know the land of such masters of literature as Flaubert and De Maupassant, the land that seemed to exercise such a charm over its visitors. I was very young and very eager as the train pulled into sight of Sacré Cœur, but I couldn't show it as I was giving polite attention to one of my shipmates in the compartment who was comparing, to its decided disadvantage, the sewerage of Paris with that of Pittsburgh.

Life in Paris for a young man is one of the few things that are better in realization than anticipation.   This is no attempt on my part to tell of a city so well known and loved by my compatriots ; it is rather an attempt to tell what Paris did to me.   I had always hated cities.   They had seemed to me the negation of beauty.   They had, I thought, stifled what was best in a man's heart and mind.   I found that in this instance I was wrong.   Here was a city of a spacious graciousness, a city which grew old with the air of a great lady.   It was a city from which escape was easy and delightful — the woods of Meudon, St. Germain, St. Cloud, and Senlis were all reasonably accessible.   I don't mean accessible as we estimate it now, but by a brief trip on the train or, better, by double-decker tram or 'bateaux mouches,' the little river boats.   Even to go to the Bois de Boulogne was an expedition, but a worth-while one.   On summer days we took a fiacre from the Rive Gauche. It ambled across the river into the bourgeois territory of the Place de la Concorde.   Sometimes the horse would proceed at a leisurely trot up the Champs Elysées, more often he walked while we admired the women and horses, the graceful façades of the private houses, now, alas ! show rooms for the Fiat and Ford.   In the Bois we played tennis at the Racing Club, lunched at Pré Catalan, lay on the grass and studied through the afternoon.   Then the long drive back in the lengthening shadows.   But such expeditions were rare ; my life usually centred about the Luxembourg gardens, the Avenue de l'Observatoire near which I lived.   Our meeting place was usually the Deux Magots on the Boulevard St. Germain rather than the Dôme and the Montparnasse area : the latter was a bit far away from my school or the Beaux Arts where most of my companions worked.

Life was stimulating and lived at an intellectual intensity that I had never imagined. For the first time, it seemed, I was thrown with a group of men deeply interested in what they were doing and ready to discuss it with passion. Talk was enormous and endless. Painters, musicians, architects, students of medicine, law or diplomacy, we all had theories and we aired those theories till dawn. But we worked, because the work was the development of the theories with which we were struggling. We worked because all around us men were working, not only with devotion, but with zeal. There was a public opinion of a sorts ; it wasn't censorious of anything but sloth or intellectual slovenliness. Drinking was all right as long as it didn't spoil your enthusiasm. Relationships with the girls of the quarter were regarded with indifference, something as normal as satisfying your hunger at lunch. The code permitted wide discretion as to the binding nature of monetary obligations. The unforgivable sin was waste of talent. I have heard condemnations uttered in cafés by men and women whom the Right Bank would regard with contempt, and the condemnations were as full of self-righteousness as a Ladies' Church Sociable. Let's not utter inanities about morality being a matter of geography. That is an absurdity which has been disproved too often to try it again. A case could be made, nevertheless, for the theory that morality is a matter of local public opinion, and that wherever a group of men and women get together, they build a sort of code for themselves and hound the transgressors with an equal enthusiasm whether they are the society of a small town in New England or the Quartier Latin at Paris.

My school, the Ecole Libre des Sciences Politiques, lay in the rue St. Guillaume, a few yards from the Boulevard St. Germain. Its faculty was astonishing : such contemporary figures as Siegfried and André Tardieu, such figures of the past as the sage of international law, Renault. When Siegfried mounted the platform the words poured from him in a torrent, he seemed impatient that the physical necessity for speech put a brake on the flow of his thoughts, he was bursting with intellectual eagerness. Tardieu's tone was more moderate, he spoke coldly and with an incisiveness of logic that could turn savage in its destructiveness. But his intellectual stimulus was unequalled. Old Renault lectured with gentle contempt, as if he was sure that he was wasting his time in dealing with low intellects such as ours. They all lectured with conviction tempered by irony, but whether the subject was law or history, politics or political economy, the lectures were lucid and terse. Their structure was logical ; careful notes of the lecture would subsequently reveal the skeleton in its entirety, from the vertebræ to the smallest joint they were carefully articulated. A wide lack in my earlier education was laid bare to me in a few weeks. I had been approximating. No one had ever driven me to exactitude of statement. There grew gradually in my mind a love of accuracy and conciseness, a hatred of vagueness and circumlocution. Above all things, thought must be pursued until it is clear to the speaker himself. He should then clothe the thought in words so simple that any child can grasp his meaning. Such was the enlightenment of French teaching. They began at the beginning, went through their story, when they came to the end, they stopped. Certainly our American education had never made me grasp the simple beauty of such presentation of thought. I began to read classic French with new purpose and found the same characteristics. What an exact language and what disciplined mentalities! I had subsequently in my office a graduate of an American university, a man of likeable personality and ability beyond the average. He would endeavor to tell me of a case on which he was working. He would begin in the middle, bewilder me with circumlocution. At the end I would have to extract the story by careful cross examination. I once told him to consider me his top sergeant and himself a corporal reporting, to return to his room, think out his report and give it to me as to a military superior. He improved beyond belief under this system, but how much easier for him if he could have had a year under French instructors and have learned his lesson there. Some time ago I was reading Wells' *Autobiography* and I came upon some lines which I might have written myself, had I been a good enough writer, to summarize what I have been trying to say in regard to French instruction. Wells is discussing Huxley's class and says — I can quote it because I have just looked up the phrase — 'It has left me that urgency for coherence, sense and consistency, that repugnance from haphazard assumptions and arbitrary statements, which is the essential distinction of the educated from the uneducated mind.'

I was not a child when I went to Paris. I was twenty-five, older than most of my comrades by two or three years, but in appearance so young that I grew a moustache for the first time to assert my manhood. But though I was older than the French lads, they had a trained intellect which I envied. They had a machine at their disposition far more serviceable than mine. Until twenty-five I had considered myself an educated man ; after twenty-five I began to work for an education.

I lived in the apartment of a painter and of a musician, Paul Renandot, and his wife Lucie. He was bald as an egg, wore a bushy black beard, lacked two front teeth and was one of the cheeriest companions I ever encountered. Under his tutelage and as my French improved, I began to savor that special light-hearted, even childish, amusement in which the Left Bank rejoices. We went to the Magic City, we slid down the Bassin des Nigauds, we danced in the streets on the 14th of July and paused to watch the fireworks on the Pont Neuf. We attended the Bal des Quatres Arts and paraded back to the Beaux Arts at dawn with a motley band in costume and out of it. We picnicked in the woods and rattled home at night on the top of the train. We watched the sun go down and the lights flicker on the Seine. They are orange and gold, green and red on a purple background, and they glimmer and sparkle as no others I know.

Paul did a lot for my taste in painting. He would never permit a visit to a museum of more than twenty minutes. He said eye and taste became tired quickly. We would visit the Louvre and the Salons but especially the Luxembourg. It was Paul's ambition to have a picture hung in the Luxembourg and he attained his ambition. Paul died in 1919 of pneumonia contracted in the last months of the war. Most of my French friends in the Sciences Politiques were killed long before that.

I followed politics, of course ; it was part of the preparation for my examinations, but I followed them academically as something too remote for personal emotion. But suddenly the Agadir incident burst on Paris. My French friends began to prepare their equipment in anticipation of mobilization orders. It was then that the threat became real and it began to dawn on my consciousness, American though I was and remote from danger, that the diplomatic moves I had been reading about had a grim reality to Europe. The sense of reality was heightened by the frankly spoken conviction, not only of my comrades, but of professors in their lectures, of the inescapability of another war with Germany. I never heard it advocated, but the fatalism with which it was regarded made a deep impression on me. It was as inevitable to them as old age and death.

I rarely visited our Embassy in Paris and only once met the Ambassador, Mr. Bacon. He delivered a lecture in admirable French at the Ecole des Sciences Politiques. I wasn't at all surprised at hearing an American Ambassador speak good French ; it seemed a normal enough requirement in that city. I did not realize how many years would pass before I heard another American Ambassador speaking French in France.

My departure from Paris was sudden, as indeed has been my departure from most posts subsequently. I received a telegram unexpectedly from Edwin Morgan, at that time our Minister in Lisbon, offering to take me on as his private secretary, saying that I had been recommended by a mutual friend. I hated to leave Paris. I hated to go without getting a diploma from the school, as I had been fascinated by the idea of donning a dress suit to appear before a board of examiners, also in dress suits, for the oral test.   Nevertheless, the best way to learn a thing was to do it, and I knew that Mr. Morgan was a man of wide experience in diplomacy so that his training would be valuable.   I accepted.

CHAPTER II

The first impression of Lisbon — I arrived late at night and tried to sleep — was noise ! Endless, varied, intermittent and prolonged. Women disputed in shrill voices, dogs barked, cats wailed, little boys fought, ash cans clattered, tram cars moaned and screamed. My verbs are exhausted, but the din was not. It continued in infinite discord throughout the night. Relative peace descended with daylight, and I sallied out tired but interested. It was all so new to me. Flagged pavements, baroque churches, a glory of flowers. Infinite color in women's dresses, mantillas covering black hair and black laughing eyes beneath. Since then I have seen dozens of South Latin cities. At that moment it was all novelty.

My chief, Mr. Morgan, put me through the round of my duties. They certainly weren't arduous, and I was delighted to find that I had time not only to continue my studies for the examinations, but to learn something of this, to me, unknown civilization. There is something dramatic and appealing about Portugal. Think of a nation which has had one great flowering of history. For a century or more at the time of Henry the Navigator they burst into world importance. Their sailors and adventurers went boldly to all portions of the globe. They charted unknown seas, discovered and claimed continents, established colonies, played one of the dominant roles in Europe. Then the relapse. For no visible reason they dwindled, their commerce shrank, their initiative disappeared,

the sons of the adventurers no longer ventured. They retained only two reminders of the past : far-flung and remote
colonies, and the distinction of being 'Great Britain's Oldest
Ally.' What caused their sudden brief flowering of brilliance ? Was it the genius of a few men ? Or was it a sudden ripening of a race reaching maturity followed by an
equally sudden decadence ? The answer is one of the riddles
of history. I tried to read Camoens to understand and to savor
the glorious past. Unhappily my knowledge of Portuguese
was never sufficient, and I did not stay long enough to master
it. So I never solved the riddle even to my own satisfaction.

Mr. Morgan had a motor, one of the few in the country at
that time. The roads were abominable but the countryside
lovely. Each week-end we took trips which remain alive in
my memory. They were venturesome as we usually had to
be assisted at some stage or other by a team of bullocks and the
local village blacksmith. One expedition is peculiarly vivid —
a trip through the Douro valley where port-wine grapes are
grown. It was late autumn, the grapes had been plucked, the
leaves of the vines had turned the steep slopes into patterns of
russet and purple. Pressing grapes was going on in the villages ; none of your grinding machines that crush the seeds and
stems, but troops of laughing girls marching around the vats,
bare legs stained purple to the thigh, singing to the guitars
they carried. The sun poured through the open door into the
dark interior of the vat rooms in a golden bar and lighted the
girls in brilliance as they passed one by one in their circuit.

The history of the Portuguese-British alliance doesn't mention it, but I am sure that the production of port wine has a lot
to do with its permanence. The Portuguese don't drink much

port ; they drink their own very decent natural wines. Nearly the whole stock of the ports is made for the British market and fashioned for the British taste. Port wine, produced in Portugal, is an exotic the world over save in Great Britain. They occasionally experiment with port wine for a limited local consumption and produce types that to my palate are superior to those bottled in Great Britain. There is a British club in Oporto at which I dined. They serve port wine for all courses from cocktail to liqueur. I remember especially a pale dry wine they served with the fish, like the finest sherry. The members of the club were British subjects whose grandfathers or great grandfathers came over with Wellington and received grants of land after the Peninsular campaign. They go 'home' to school and the university and are more British than anything outside of India.

Shortly before my arrival a revolution had dislodged the monarchy, and the several governments in power during my stay arrived by violence and departed by the same road. The coups d'état were seldom bloody though I have seen cannon firing down the Avenida to the damage of the Wagon-Lit Hotel.

One night I was dining in a balcony above the public square. The place was seething, with an excited crowd milling about and listening to harangues by vociferous orators. Suddenly some fellow hurled a paving stone through a druggist's window. The crash of glass stilled the crowd into an instantaneous hush. As if they had been awaiting the signal, trumpets blared from the plaza entrances directly below us, a company of cavalry trotted into the square, wheeled into line and moved against the crowd with drawn swords. The people broke and scampered out the farther end of the square and in five minutes the place was deserted save for the cavalry. We felt as if we had had balcony seats at a singularly convincing mob scene. There wasn't a single casualty.

To add to the distress of the short-lived governments, the followers of Manoel, the legitimate King, and of Miguel, the pretender, were causing continuous trouble. They used to gather on Spanish territory, preferably on the northern frontier, rush across the line, shoot up a village, chase out the loyal guard, and retire before troops could be brought up to retaliate for the raid. Nobody had thought of a "non-intervention" committee in those days and people were much more lenient towards 'volunteers.' It was supposed in Lisbon that the Spanish Government was favorable towards either Manoel or Miguel, I don't remember which, and that it was useless to protest against the raids. So all they could do was to chase them. We joined in the chase. Mr. Morgan was as keen as I was so we drove his car to the frontier time and again when we heard either that raids were in process or contemplated. The nearest we came was to reach a burning village the raiders had abandoned. We never caught up with them or really witnessed a raid. This to our great regret. Our nerves had not become jaded by a world war and episodes such as these were of thrilling interest.

I made few friends in Lisbon. The people whom I would have met socially in normal times had closed their houses and left the capital. In many cases they had fled the country. Those people were in sympathy with the monarchy and had taken shelter through the series of domestic upheavals. Men in the government had a too precarious tenure of office to indulge in social diversion, and, in any case, governments were so short-lived that there was barely time to get acquainted with the new ministry.

Thus I had to seek other diversion and found it waiting. I became an *aficionado* or ardent fan of the bull fights. To my surprise, the fights were bloodless, the bulls were not killed. The *picadores* were mounted on thoroughbreds and deep disgrace fell on the man who allowed the bull to touch his horse. When the bull was tired and had reached the point where in Spain the *matador* delivers the death stroke, a curious procedure was followed to put the bull out of action. A band of men formed a wedge with a stout fellow at the apex. They moved slowly at the bull which awaited the attack snorting and pawing the ground. At a distance of perhaps two yards the bull attacked. The stout fellow threw himself between the horns, wrapping his arms around the bull's neck, blinding him with his body. His companions seized the bull, tripped and tied him. He was then dragged off in a cloud of dust. Portuguese bull-fighting was full of stunts. A man clothed in scarlet awaited the bull's attack with his arms folded. The bull would charge him and stop short when the man did not move. He would approach him slowly with every sign of puzzlement, sniff at the man and turn away in disgust. There was a band of pole-vaulters who would run at the bull when he charged, plant the pole in the ground and rise in the air. The bull's rush carried away the pole and the acrobat dropped behind the animal's tail.

Bull fights in Portugal were radically different from those in Spain, but they had many points in common. The scene was similar, blazing sun on a gaily colored crowd, the preparatory fanfare of trumpets, the stately parade of the performers in brilliant silken costumes. The same tactics of the men with *capas*, the same teasing of the bull by the *banderilleros*, but here the resemblance stopped. The essential characteristic of the fights in Lisbon was bloodlessness, horses were not gored nor bulls killed. The crowds went equally wild. At any misstep or failure in tactic, they would howl and demand the blood of the performer, threatening his life as an American crowd in a baseball game does that of the umpire. Their enthusiasm for good performance was boundless.

There is a lot to learn about bull-fighting before the observer really begins to appreciate it. When an American goes for the first time, he gets about the same proportion of the game as if he were seeing a cricket match or as if an Englishman were watching baseball. When later I saw fights in Madrid I was choked with the horror of blood spilling. Nevertheless I was thrilled by the stately mechanism of a performance in which beauty and grace are accompanied by imminent danger of being mauled. Hemingway tells of this contrast between danger and beauty. *Death in the Afternoon* is the great epic of the spectacle, at least in English. I have not seen a fight in many years but it seems fair to add that I am told that in the last dozen years the horses of the *picadores* have been so padded that there is much less bloodshed than formerly.

I never really became a part of Portugal, or Portugal of me. Perhaps my stay there and my visits to Spain gave me a better comprehension of Latin America when I reached it. Portugal was remote from my interests, the problems of the Iberian Peninsula did not impinge to a great extent on the policies of Europe. The Portuguese were giving thought to their internal problems only and it was hard for an outsider to feel a passionate interest in whether one or another group ran the nation. Perhaps my stay was too brief. I did, however, develop a liking and deep respect for the Portuguese peasant, cheerful, industrious, honest, and polite. His most outstanding characteristic is his natural dignity. He enjoys himself with cheerfulness but always with a sense of self-respect. His village dances and his diversions are picturesque and colorful, but his dignity is never lost. He is after all a close relation to the peasant of Spain whom I have heard described as the 'real nobility' of that land. The peasant remains a sympathetic memory. He typifies to me the virtues and stability of that land far more than the excited crowds of the capital.

The examinations for the diplomatic service were to take place in Washington late in the autumn of 1911. I took leave of Mr. Morgan with real regret. He had taken endless trouble to train me in detail, and the example of his technique with foreign officials has often been useful. His was a strange nature. He loathed any form of exercise and was quite frank in expressing his distaste. He was gregarious without being friendly. A poor linguist, nevertheless he had the faculty, which Mr. Herrick in Paris had so abundantly, of winning the respect and liking of people to whom he couldn't talk. He knew his job and did his best to teach it to me. I had no claim on him and was grateful for his kindness.

Washington again for my examinations. The written tests were exhausting, but they were only different in degree from what I had become accustomed to in school and university. The oral tests were a real ordeal. It is not easy to appear before a jury of five or six senior men in the service and do your-self justice.   As I went into the room for my turn, I happened to think of the 'Card' in a book of that name by Arnold Ben-nett.   When the 'Card' wanted to nerve himself to some piece of incredible effrontery, he would say to himself, 'They can't eat me.'   I found the phrase really consoling in presenting myself.   For, after all, it is a piece of effrontery to appear be-fore a lot of gentlemen with years of experience in foreign af-fairs and say to them in effect, 'See here, I can convince you that I am material to become even as you, or better.' Anyhow, they were exceedingly polite and asked, to my surprise, ques-tions that demanded thought and careful presentation, rather than a knowledge of fact.   With one exception : I was re-quested to name the capitals and the states appertaining thereto from the Rio Grande to Panama.   Fortunately, everybody in Washington who was interested knew that one member of the examining board never omitted this question.

I have sat on many examining boards since and have watched young men present themselves.   They have had my deep sympathy.   I have discussed and reflected at length upon the type of examination, and can see no better form than the present unless we are to enter upon almost prohibitive ex-penditure.   There must be some way in which the examiners can convince themselves that the candidate can keep cool un-der strain, can use his faculties in oral conversation in un-expected situations.   Therefore, unless we establish a real government school for the foreign service and select the candidates therefrom, I can see no way of bettering the pres-ent situation.   The school would be ideal, the masters could learn the characteristics of the various men through a considerable period and could avoid many of the mistakes that are now inevitable through our summary method of selection. Character, coolness, quick response to critical tests could all be assessed as well as scholastic attainments.   I say the school would be ideal, but with the small numbers which we can admit yearly to the service, the per capita cost of education would be prohibitive.

It is not easy to enumerate the characteristics and to describe the temperament that make a good foreign service officer.   There must be a considerable degree of education.   It is essential that the officer be able to converse on an equal footing with men of all types with whom he must come into contact in his posts abroad, that he have a mind trained for the assimilation and understanding of new customs and civilizations, and that he have a real taste for study.   It is unlikely that a candidate can have these characteristics without at least a university education, and the outstanding successes in the service have been made by men of a considerable degree of training beyond the university.   Needless to say, the candidate must be possessed of habits, manners, and character which will fit him to represent our country among foreign peoples and to show to them an example of what is best in America.   He must be loyal and be willing to subordinate himself to his superiors even when he may not find them likeable.   It will take years, in all probability, before he can act on his own.   He must have a spirit of co-operation.   Too great individualism of action does not fit into a great organization like the State Department although individualism of spirit and mentality are the highest of assets.   He must have patience, for in no other profession are the successes gained to the same degree by patient and long continued effort. Finally, he must have the quality of making men like him and trust him, that elusive quality which for want of a better word we call tact.

The foreign service officer must have, in addition to the positive quality, a negative or self-denying quality as well. He must remain non-partisan in the internal affairs of his country. By its very nature, the foreign service officer must be and is non-partisan, and the men of the service must and do give the same loyalty and service to any chief, whatever his politics. Men in the service do not know, as a rule, whether another member has inclinations on one side or the other. We are seldom home at elections and scrupulously avoid partisan comment during an election or at any other time. Our long periods of absence from the United States give us a certain detachment of view on internal politics, and we realize, one and all, that on our scrupulous non-partisanship depends, in a large measure, the future of the service.

I have written earlier of the condition of the service up to the early years of the century. To all of us who serve in it, it is the highest satisfaction to compare our foreign representation now with that of the past. The service has faults and failures, most of which can be eradicated with the friendly help of Congress and of the Administration, but generally speaking, the past thirty years have seen an American service built up, slowly but surely, of which we have real reason to be proud and which in its rank and file is certainly the equal and perhaps the superior of that of any other country.

Those few days in Washington are memorable to me in one respect which far outweighs the memory of my examinations.

I made the acquaintance of my wife, Katherine Bogle, and heard her sing in the house of Mrs. Lawrence Townsend. She sang 'Le Prophête,' 'Délilah' and 'Im wunderschönen Monat Mai,' I remember.

I awaited in Chicago the results of the examinations. I thought I had done well, but between confidence and certainty there is a wide gap, especially when one really cares about the result. At last the telegram arrived which notified me I was going to Guatemala, the same telegram that I wrote about in the opening lines of this story. It is literally true that I knew no more then about that country than the sketchy outline which I remember from the encyclopedia. I have just taken down the Britannica as a matter of curiosity. It prints pages about Guatemala : flora and fauna, history, finance, a thousand details. Whether a deeper interest explains the voluminous information in the Britannica, or whether that evening years ago I pulled out a mediocre encyclopedia, I do not know. But I recall the excited conjecture in my brother's house that night as to what sort of land I was going to.

When I came to say good-bye to Chicago and the North Shore I realized for the first time how much I was leaving, in spite of the fact that I left gladly and voluntarily. It suddenly came to me that childhood friends and surroundings are irreplaceable, and that whatever relationships one forms subsequently, the earliest ones are the most enduring and probably the most satisfying. Thank goodness, they endure and can be picked up readily. At each visit to the United States I return to Chicago. I have a sister in Evanston, a brother in Winnetka, and a sister-in-law in Lake Forest. All along the line of the Shore and in the city itself are people that I rejoice to see and talk with, people for whom I have an abiding affection that time does not dissolve. These friends are of permanent satisfaction. They lead delightful lives. They have wide interests. The atmosphere is as stimulating as any I know. The city itself has become beautiful and has so become through conscious and determined effort on the part of my friends. I am proud that I belong to this part of the world. It may even be that my long absences have led me to appreciate it more than those who live at home.

I had to return to Washington again for a month to be prepared for the post to which I was going. All who had been successful in the examinations had been ordered back. Richard Pennoyer, Albert Ruddock, and I shared an apartment in the old Shoreham and the whole month was rare fun. Albert's marriage took place during this period. The incoming class gave him a dinner, for which Albert eventually paid, if I remember rightly, and to which we invited all those in the Department who had been particularly concerned with our instruction. We had prepared a lot of jests at the expense of our teachers which we found extraordinarily humorous, a sort of minor gridiron dinner. A feeling of partnership in the organization began to grow, together with the knowledge that these men that I began to like so much would be my companions in my profession and would, I hoped, become my friends. It was fascinating to see the State Department from the inside, but it was a deceptive picture. Never again was I to see it in its remote and traditional atmosphere of leisure. Never again did I see its occupants clad in cutaway coats as a normal badge of office.

CHAPTER III

As I write of Guatemala, I shall start, as do all orthodox memoirs, with a bibliography. For this purpose we can consider the area south of Texas to the Panama Canal as a unit. Books written about any part apply in essentials to any other part. The same low-lying east coast, the same mighty range of the Cordillera with its abrupt and glorious slope to the Pacific, give the various nations a certain physical resemblance. The same industrious picturesque Indian gives the villages similar characteristics ; the same church and the same civilization influenced the architecture of the towns. The same spirit of grave courtesy prevails among the people ; anywhere in this land you may meet a *caballero* riding his mule along a dusty road. His saddle and bridle will be finished in silver. He will be clad in wide hat, blue tattered jacket and worn canvas trousers, his bare feet bound with large silver spurs. The silver mounted butt of his revolver will peep from its holster. When you ask him a question he sweeps off his hat, climbs down to the dusty road, and puts himself at your complete disposition. In this part of the world national boundaries mean little change to the eyes of a foreigner.

The first writer on my list is O. Henry, whose works are known to every American reader. He has had few rivals in English for the mastery of the short story. Hundreds of criticisms have been written ; they have not yet, to my mind, done him justice. Many of his stories are laid in Central

America. They smell of Central America, but they treat of the exotic and the bizarre of Central America. His stories are essentially true. I know the people he writes of. I knew General Lee Christmas and General Drummond. I knew the fruit company agents and the local vice-consuls. I knew the exiled German, Englishman, American of the tropical low-lying East Coast. Nevertheless, O. Henry tells of the foreigner in Central America, and especially of the flamboyant, venturesome fellow who sought those lands for freedom, danger and adventure. They were the exceptions; while the type was common enough, they remain exceptions. The more honor to O. Henry. He was not interested in writing a guide book ; he was interested in human beings and the more picturesque the human being, and the more he deviates from type, the greater O. Henry's interest. But you wouldn't get a characterization of Chicago from a memoir of Al Capone. Nor do you get a picture of the real Central America from the books of O. Henry.

One writer, and I know one only, has caught the spirit of this region. Flandreau in *Viva Mexico* writes with affection and understanding. He is sensible to beauty, humor, pathos, and the lives of the peoples of Central America are abundantly full of all three. His scene of the family getting ready to go to market is repeated in thousands of houses and huts. The book is masterly. It is the classic in English for these lands.

There remains a book of a quite different type. The writer is Bérnal Diaz de Castillo, a subordinate officer of Cortez and Alvarado. When Cortez had finished his amazing conquest of Mexico he directed his lieutenant, Alvarado, to march to the south, to the greater glory of the King of Spain, and to save the souls of the heathen in that region. Alvarado made an expedition and conquests as astounding as those of his chief. When one travels through the lands he marched over, one is amazed at the endurance and perseverance of the conquistadores. Clad in helmets and armor, they roasted in their steel jackets, they crossed swamps and deserts, they lived on the land and in repeated battles they fought enemies fifty and a hundred times as numerous. When the battles were over, the conquests assured, Bérnal Diaz de Castillo was rewarded for his services by the grant of a farm in Guatemala. He took to himself an Indian wife and proceeded to write his memoirs. He was simple, devout, and honest. As soon as I came across the story I am about to relate I knew that Bérnal Diaz was an historian to whom full trust could be given. It appears that at one stage of their adventures — I believe it was near the Lake of Atitlán — the Spaniards were sorely beset by their adversaries, who numbered fifty to one against them. The battle was going badly and the Spaniards were being slowly pressed back when St. Iago appeared on a white horse with a gleaming sword and led the weary Spaniards into a final assault. They overthrew the enemy and pushed several thousand of them over the cliff into the lake. Here Bérnal Diaz remarks (I am only quoting approximately and from memory), 'I was not a man of sufficient virtue, or a Christian good enough that the sight of this miracle should be vouchsafed me. Nevertheless I know it is true because my companions who saw it have told me.'

My bibliography of Guatemala is not extensive, but you must admit it is varied. Guatemala itself exercises an influence which makes the written word superfluous for those who have visited it.   How many times in my life I have discovered in talking to a stranger that he had been to Guatemala.   Each time as I learned this fact I felt a glow of interest and could see from the quick smile on the other's face that he felt as I did.   Guatemala is a bond to those who know it ; many a gathering has had to listen to tales of the country when two or more friends of Guatemala come together.   There is a vividness, a freshness about our memories which time does not dim and other impressions do not efface.

The boat from New Orleans tied up at the wharf at Puerto Barrios on the east coast of Guatemala before dawn.   I went up on deck in the black moist night of the tropics.   A voice called my name and in the companion-way light the captain said, 'This is Victor Cutter of the United Fruit Company.'   I shook hands with a huge figure in tropic white ; I noticed a broad grin on a rugged clean-shaven face, an abruptness of manner which hid a certain shyness which he would never admit, even to himself.   Cutter's name will often appear in these pages.   He was the last person to say good-bye to me at Puerto Barrios as well as the first to greet me.   He was picturesque.   O. Henry would have cherished him.   A graduate of Dartmouth, he learned the business of banana growing and negro management in Costa Rica, gained the confidence of Minor Keith, Central America's almost legendary figure in banana growing and railroad building, and was promoted to be manager of the newly opened plantations in Guatemala.   His handling of negroes was remarkable.   He excelled in everything they admired.   He could fight the wildest of them, he could outshoot them, his endurance was unlimited and his occasional flash of ferocious temper kept them cowed.   Such qualities were necessary. These negroes from Jamaica were cheerful and reasonably industrious, but full of liquor they became dangerous. Cutter would face them down in their worst moments. I stood up with him at his wedding and still see him occasionally when I go to Boston. He became President and later Chairman of the Board of the United Fruit Company. He has kept the grin, the abrupt manner and, I suppose, the willingness to bash a buck negro should the latter become drunk and obstreperous.

Cutter led me down the dock. We passed another boat tied to the wharf taking on a load of bananas. Bananas bruise so easily that they cannot be loaded by machine. A line of negroes stripped to the waist and bare-footed, each bent under the load of a huge bunch, strode up the wharf, mounted the gang plank under the yellow flare of two resinous torches, passed their burden into the hold through a chain gang of handlers. At the head of the gang plank, the blackest and biggest buck of all smoked a cigarette and whirled a machete. His teeth gleamed white and a yellow handkerchief knotted about his head reflected the flames of the torches. Each carrier gripped his bunch with his right hand close to his shoulder ; if the stem projecting from his hand was too long, the guardian of the gang plank made a quick negligent flick of his machete and lopped off the unnecessary length of stem. The blade passed two inches in front of the carrier's nose and one inch in front of his fingers. I stared at it, fascinated, and winced each time the knife flickered. The negroes softly crooned a song as they approached the flickering light, their bare feet made no sound, the swish of the machete was audible, and the bump on the planks of the severed ends.

My train for the capital left at dawn, ran through jungle for
a while, then pushed out into the banana lands, a sea of them.
They seemed to reach the horizon.   Hours of hot, dusty desert came.   We passed Zapata — now, I understand, the junc-
tion of the railroad to Salvador.   Towards the end of the afternoon the train began to puff in labor.   We mounted heavily
wooded hills by zigzag ascents and ran into the capital just as
darkness was coming on.

My chief, Reynolds Hitt, took me to his house for dinner.
Reynolds had had a lot of training as Secretary and Counselor
in various posts before he became Minister.   He was most
helpful to me.   Especially in form of correspondence, his advice has been useful to me for years.   One of the standing re-
proaches to my profession is that it is interested in form and
not in substance.   This is occasionally true but only occasionally.   A knowledge of form is nevertheless of the highest
value, especially in a profession where form has become traditional and where substance clothed in improper form can not
only give offense, but can be even dangerous.   His wife,
Edith, was a joy.   A mass of shining fair hair, a charming and
humorous face, a flashing smile, Edith talked with a drawl that
hid the alertness of her humor.   Her French was fluent, but
the slow softly spoken phrases used in a language of staccato
terseness gave an exotic air to the tongue and spiced the comedy of what she told.   In the brief time that they were in
Guatemala with me I saw them constantly.   I wasn't invited
to meals ; I was expected.   We would lunch together on the
veranda covered portion of the patio, the sun poured on the
flowers, the fountain splashed.   A few guests might be present, but lunch was never formal.   We talked and smoked

and laughed until we returned reluctantly and tardily to the Chancery.

Shortly after my arrival Mr. Knox paid an official visit. It was the first time, I believe, that an American Secretary of State had come to that part of the world and the excitement was tremendous. A special train from the West Coast brought the Secretary's party. The entire population of the town was in the streets to receive him, and he drove to the residence put at his disposal through lines of children bearing flowers. I have a confused memory of parades of bare-footed soldiers in dusty blue uniforms, of huge dinners, and of balls where the blonde American women made a tremendous sensation. All was excitement and enthusiasm.

A day or two before Mr. Knox reached the capital, Katherine Elkins, Billy Hitt, Reynolds' brother, and Stephen Elkins and his wife turned up to visit the Hitts. So we had not only balls and ceremonies, but a most hilarious time by ourselves. We went on picnics and horseback excursions. We played tennis. We swam in a pool at Esquintla where the sun poured through the overhanging leaves and dappled the water in golden green patches to match the bamboo groves about the edges.

The Hitts remained only a short time after my arrival, but they were joyous weeks and so stay vivid. The only train running east left at six in the morning. Nevertheless most of the city got out of bed to speed the departure of the Minister and his wife. Their private car was hitched to the end of the train, and I can see it now as it pulled out, Reynolds and Edith waving from the back platform where masses of flowers left them barely room to stand.

In the meantime I had been finding a house. They were not easy to get, especially with our American conception of bathrooms, and as for furniture, the less said about the specimens I was offered the better. I finally found one, a tiny house belonging to an elderly Scotch couple who were returning home for an indefinite visit. For plumbing it had the one indispensable necessity, but no bath. The improvised bath was a circular rubber contrivance. The servants had to dip up water in huge jars from the 'pila' (a sort of pool where the washing was done), heat it on the stove and bring it on order. If you were an acrobat with an adequate sponge you could wash all over, but there was no way of getting under water as the bath could only be filled to a depth of about four inches.

A daughter of the house had painted water colors, so the salon was a horror. It was so bad there was nothing to do with it and I lived in my bedroom and a tiny smoking room. I remember I brought Edith Hitt to see the house after I had signed the contract. She gave one horrified look at the drawing room and became extremely polite. But the patio had charm and I lived there when the weather permitted. Orchids were abundant and cheap. It soon became known that I liked them and the Indians who came to market from the country got in the habit of bringing great baskets and sprays to me and selling them for derisive prices. The house had, of course, no heating arrangements so I installed a small electric heater in the smoking room. It was all I ever needed.

This leads me on to the climate of Guatemala. I found it ideal. It was never very hot in the capital — it lies some 5000 feet high. We played tennis and rode horseback the year round. One wore a white suit during daylight in the hot season, but changed or put on an overcoat in the evening. During the rains the country was at its most beautiful. The rain obligingly waited as a rule until 3:30 p.m. so one rode in the morning in brilliant sunshine and worked late. Indeed, it was a hardy person who ventured out in the rain ; when it came it was a deluge ! The stone-flagged streets sloped steeply to a central gutter, and in five minutes the gutter was a raging torrent. They put up little wooden bridges, draw-bridges which were down during the rain and open in dry weather. Where bridges were lacking, patient Indians waited under their ponchos and carried you across piggyback for a couple of cents.

Then I had to get servants. Old-timers in Guatemala had told me never to accept any servant that wore shoes or, in the case of women, had their hair done up. With either of these two characteristics, they said, the servants considered themselves 'caballeros' and ladies, and their value as servants was nil. In my own mind I put the old-timers in the same category as ladies the world over who have foretold to me the horrors of revolution because shop-girls wear silk stockings.

So when a young man in immaculate white suit and shoes presented himself to apply for the job as butler I had no prejudice against him, was impressed with his delightful voice and easy grace and hired him on the spot. I explained he was to be butler-valet. He replied that it was perhaps inconsistent with his dignity to be a valet but that he felt that his friends would not look down upon him for undertaking this service since he was assisting in a 'distinguished diplomatic household.' So everything was charming. Fernando was a valet of exceptional deftness. He loved clothes so much himself that he kept mine in excellent condition. His graceful hospitality with a cocktail tray warmed the hearts of all arrivals. His presence serving at the table gave a distinction to my dinners that none of my guests could bring.   I went away for a few days and on my return Fernando did not open the door. The other servants explained that he was ill so I went to the hospital, took him out of the common ward and had him given the best care and attention.   Fernando came back, entered the room where I was sitting, kissed my hand before I could prevent him and with tears in his eyes said, 'Sir, you have been so good to me I could thank you on my knees.   I have re-flected if there is any way within my limited power to thank you, and can think of only one thing — to restore you this.' 'This' was a ruby stick-pin that he had purloined from my dresser.   Fernando fell sick again and I talked with his doctor who told me that he could no longer live at that altitude and must depart for the lowlands.   So I called up Cutter in the banana lands who, on my warm recommendation, took Fer-nando as his butler.   Some weeks later I encountered Cutter in the capital and asked for news of Fernando.   Cutter began to laugh.   'He was the best servant I ever had but my wife fired him.   She said it made her nervous to be served by a butler clad in silk shirts with H. R. W.' (my initials) 'em-broidered on the sleeve.'

So I reverted to barefooted females with hair down their back.   One of them was a cook, and what a cook !   Juana had been employed in an American family before coming to me and had learned all there was of the best of our southern cooking.   I should like to have dined at the house of her mis-tress ; it must have been superlative.   I became acquainted with a Spaniard in Guatemala who invited me to dinner.

When I appreciated his food he sent his cook around to instruct Juana in various Spanish and French dishes of which she had never heard but which she acquired with the ready aptitude of the born artist.   The Spaniard, Roderigo Dominguez, was a much older man.   He became interested in me and proceeded to instruct me in his philosophy of life.   It was a sort of hedonism in practical application.   He once said to me, 'Young man, by the age of forty-five you will have learned that there is only one joy in life that you can really count on, that of the palate.   The Good God gives us food and drink twice or three times a day, and it is a blessing of Heaven that we can count upon and look forward to this unfailing joy so often.'   He taught me a lot.   He taught me that perfection of cooking does not lie in combinations and complications ; that it lies in the simplest things, beautifully handled.   Witness the lowly string-bean.   Can anything be more horrible when it is carelessly cooked ?   Can anything surpass it when it is properly done in France ?   He taught me about wine.   I learned from him that wine is at its best when it is natural.   That the bubbles in champagne prevent the palate from performing its task of appreciation.   That nothing which has been doctored can give the same satisfaction as good vintages of Bordeaux, Burgundy, and the wines of the Rhine Valley.   Dominguez did not toil, neither did he spin.   He played a little music, not much.   He ate his food and drank his drink.   He enjoyed them both in anticipation, in contemplation, and in memory. His life was very full.

My house lay on Fourth Street around the corner from Third Avenue, South.   The streets were identical.   The houses were generally one story, adobe walls tinted in pastel

shades, iron-barred windows, tiled roofs. It was only occasionally, when one of the heavy front doors was left open,
that one glimpsed the cool green and bright flowers of the
patios. Motors were almost unknown, the streets were too
bad and roads in the country almost non-existent. In the late
afternoon the two or three cars in the city, owned by wealthy
families, paraded solemnly out to the Reforma, a sort of park
near the town, turned around and paraded as solemnly back.
The streets looked deserted normally, the only figures some
Indians leading goats, carrying baskets. Occasionally a 'caballero' on horse or mule, more rarely still, a carriage with two
horses clattered over the stone flags, carrying some lady out
on her calls.

The show place of the town was the Plaza, bordered by the
Cathedral, the Presidential palace, and a military barracks.
The Plaza was the centre of church fiestas, military demonstrations and governmental ceremonial. Here in the cool of the
evening the girls walked around while the lads of the village
looked them over and discussed them as they moved around in
the opposite direction. To a man accustomed to more northern cities, a town built under Spanish influence has an in-
hospitable atmosphere, no green lawns, no trees, barred windows. Each house looks like a miniature fortress, and indeed
that is what it is. At the first sign of political disturbance the
citizen bars the door, closes his shutters behind his iron grating
and abides with his family until the rivals have shot it out.
The great earthquake of 1917 demolished a portion of the
city. I do not know if it still preserves its classic Spanish type.

The outskirts of the town are surpassingly beautiful. Riding was a never-failing joy ; I could have charted the region

for twenty miles around. The great plateau is bounded by mountains and itself split into deep 'barrancas' or ravines, tremendous and sudden water courses during the rains. Often I would ride to the western edge of the plateau to a point where, emerging from the woods, the sudden vision lay before me of the western slope of the Cordillera. The Pacific was clearly visible, a thin white line of surf edged the deep blue. From there to my feet every shade of green sprang from the different vegetation. Sugar first, a deep rich green, shimmered under the tropic sun. A band of coffee plantations showed still more darkly ; it glistened and turned copper as one looked at it longer. Then came maize and grain, lighter again and showing more movement in the gentle breeze. Above me on the slopes, the black green of fir forests and away off the gleaming snow of the great volcanos. If the Bon Dieu decides that my life has been worthy and asks what sort of region I should prefer for the hereafter I shall reply that I want to be with a chosen band of friends on the western slope of the Cordillera.

On the west coast lies the so-called port of San José, a small town built on the edge of the beach facing the eternal surf of the Pacific. The water deepens swiftly ; bathing is a tricky business as the surf is so heavy that the swimmer must dive through every wave or be rolled about and badly mauled. An iron pier runs out to deep water and offers landing facilities of a primitive sort to lighters from the boats anchored beyond the surf and rolling ceaselessly in the swell. Sharks are abundant and we used to fish for them with lines from the pier.

The Western Railroad descends the slope to link the capital with San José. It curls down the slope in a series of hair-pin turns steeper than anything I have seen outside of cog-wheel roads in Switzerland. The little locomotive works as hard going down to check the speed as it does to pull up the train on the return voyage. Before I got there a couple of workmen who lived half way down the slope got drunk and decided to take a free ride home. They stole a flat workmen's car, the kind that works by pushing handles up and down. They pushed it off the brink and disappeared singing into the night. They must have attained a vertiginous speed. Before they even reached their home the car charged through a cattle gate that had been swung across the line. The next day it was apparent that the car had charged through the gate, but the workmen had not gone with it. They remained on the gate, and report says they had to be scraped off.

CHAPTER IV

I was Chargé d'Affaires of the United States of America. I spoke with my own voice as representative of the United States. In those days of 'Dollar Diplomacy' and in those regions the voice of the United States was the voice of Jove. My lightest word in conversation was debated and discussed. Hidden meanings were searched out and a degree of cunning and omniscience attributed which was too often without basis, hence doubly flattering. For nearly two years I was without a Chief and wielded an authority and carried a responsibility of which I was more conscious than of any I have subsequently borne. I was twenty-six years old and like the big frog in the little pond, the pond was my world, and I never considered its dimensions.

American and British diplomats the world over are in turn amused, irritated, and aghast at the reverberations which the expression of their personal opinions will call forth. Our governments and our diplomats are supposed to have far-seeing and uncannily intelligent plans, reaching into the future to an object months and years in the distance. Unless I am mistaken, it was Sir Edward Grey who discussed this question in his memoirs and who remarked that during his term of office he was so pressed that he could not remember having taken any step that was not of immediate urgency and for the solving of a problem directly in front of him. Whether other governments make and adhere to projects of such dimensions and requiring such foresight and wisdom I have never been able to find out. Perhaps it is merely the bewilderment of the Latin mind at the system of trial and error that the Anglo-Saxon instinctively uses. Our approach to a question is rarely one of considered logic, hence it must be really bewildering to others.

Manuel Estrada Cabrera had been President fourteen years since his election in 1898. In 1906 General Barillas had attempted a revolution and Honduras, Salvador, and Costa Rica joined forces with him. But the United States had used its good offices to restore peace, and the Central American treaties of 1907 had resulted from the ensuing negotiations. The story was told me in Guatemala that the American negotiators were finding it difficult to bring the opposing parties to an agreement. Accordingly, the American representatives invited the hostile delegates to a dinner on board an American cruiser at anchor in the Pacific. None of the Central Americans had been afloat before, and the effect of the Pacific swell on a boat at anchor will make the most hardened seaman squeamish. Very little further pressure was needed, the story goes, to make the delegates sign an agreement and hurry back to dry land.

Estrada Cabrera was fifty-five years old when I first knew him. In appearance he was pure Indian, a thick-set swarthy figure, though his Spanish indicated a degree of education, and his poetry, in which he delighted, was of no little merit. This statement, I hasten to add, I make on the authority of better judges than myself. At first I used to visit him with an interpreter, but as my Spanish improved, I could talk to him directly and came to know him better.

Estrada had a sense of humor, a well charted political course, and a philosophy of government which he had worked out entirely by himself as I never heard him cite a book or author. His guiding principle of policy was never to be at odds with the United States. He was convinced that a knowledge on the part of his people that the United States was friendly to him made one of the best guarantees for his security in office. He once said to me, 'Huerta' (the Dictator of Mexico at the time) 'cannot endure. He has offended the Government of the United States. He has thus violated the first rule of behavior for a dictator of the Caribbean area.' Estrada Cabrera was a genius in procrastination, in the use of every device of constitutional government for delay, in spite of the fact that the constitution and all forms of government functioned in strict accord with his orders. Nevertheless if he became finally convinced that the American Government was seriously interested in a matter, he inevitably met us. I never knew him to violate his own rule of the dictator's behavior. He had no faith in the ability of his own people to govern themselves ; some of his best humor was at the expense of democratic government in Guatemala.

Several years before my arrival there had been a serious attempt on the life of Estrada Cabrera. The Cadet Corps was made up of young men, really boys, of good family. It was the smartest organization in the Republic. A conspiracy was hatched among the cadets to assassinate the President as he came out of the Palace to take his carriage for some ceremony. The cadets were drawn up at 'present arms' awaiting his descent. He appeared at the door accompanied by Baron von Merck, a German whom he kept by him as a sort of watch-dog. The boys opened fire. The President, slightly wounded, flung himself to the pavement. Von Merck stood astride of him with a revolver in each hand. He killed several of the cadets, the rest broke and fled in a panic. Estrada Cabrera retaliated dreadfully. The boys were relentlessly hunted down, some killed on the spot, many torn from their families, who have had no news of them to this day. They simply vanished.

The better class families of the capital hated the President bitterly, but the hatred was tempered by fear, and in some cases I encountered, even by a reluctant admiration. There were things to admire about the man. He had preserved order in a region accustomed to disorder. He had encouraged railroad building and investment. Trade flourished. He had established a wide-spread system of compulsory primary education on a race of illiterates. His people had prospered, even if they had no voice in the government. Estrada Cabrera should be numbered among the great dictators of the Caribbean region. In his smaller sphere, he ranks with Porfirio Diaz. But he played fewer favorites than the latter ; a lonely man, he ruled by fear alone. After the attempted assassination, he made few public appearances and even then was heavily guarded. He lived alone in his palace, he ate alone. According to rumor such was his fear of poison that he ate only food prepared by his mother. He was eventually deposed and died a prisoner in his own country place outside the city. He met a more tranquil end than his career seemed to promise and than that encountered by most dictators of the region.

Toledo Herrarte, Doctor of Medicine, was the Minister for Foreign Affairs. His French was fluent, his intelligence acute, but one sensed in every conversation that he took no decision of importance, but like the fox terrier in the advertisement, he

listened for 'his master's voice.' Adrián Recinos, the Under-
Secretary, now Minister to Washington, was a different man
altogether. Modest, unassuming, but of considerable intelligence and learning, he frequently visited me in my house, and
I enjoyed his companionship.

The work in the Legation dealt mainly with what are known
as 'protection of interest' cases. It was rarely unduly arduous
though on occasion not without excitement. The only really
laborious period I went through was when the clerk of the
Legation, my friend Carlos Palma, fell sick. This happened
at a busy period, and I was compelled to do everything but
sweep out the office. The accounts bothered me most. I
would do them, then carry them to Palma's bedside for check-
ing. The detail of an office has never since held any insuper-
able mysteries. The work could be arranged to suit any taste,
certainly to suit mine. There was only one boat each week
from New Orleans. It reached Puerto Barrios at the end of
the week, thus the diplomatic pouch was in the office on Monday morning. All the travellers on that boat would have
called and stated their business, if any, by Wednesday. By
Thursday afternoon, by pushing hard, I could be through with
the visitors and with the work brought by the pouch, free to
mount my mule for a long week-end trip of exploration or
visiting in plantations or 'fincas' as they are called in that part
of the world. There was little chance of interruption. Washington was more remote then to that near-by post than it is
now to Siam. Cable messages were rare. There was no telephone, no airplane, and letters from Washington came only by
pouch as we never used the open mail. When I went on an

expedition, I arranged with Palma a series of code words he could telegraph me in case of emergency.   They ranged from 'Think it advisable to return,' to 'Gallop all the way.'

I remember the case of van Jennings, a naturalized American who had visited Guatemala before my arrival, returned to America where he had written and published violent attacks on Estrada Cabrera.   He became the agent of a piano company and made the mistake of returning to Guatemala. Hardly had he set foot in the country when he was seized, his luggage sealed and sent to the capital.   There an examination was made of his effects.   Parts of piano mechanism that he was carrying as samples were declared pieces of an infernal machine.   He was clapped into prison and held for trial for conspiring against the life of the President.   He wrote me daily from prison saying that the guards left his door open so that he would attempt to escape and could then be shot in the back under 'ley de fuga.'   He wrote on wrapping paper, toilet paper, the tail of a shirt ; his dossier was packed with the strangest missives.   As this case was of personal interest to the President, I knew that nothing could be done through the Foreign Office.   I went to Estrada Cabrera repeatedly and finally extracted a promise that a presidential pardon would be issued after condemnation.   Then I spent my time in a strange activity for an American representative.   I pushed with every resource at my command to obtain the rapid condemnation of an American citizen.   Van Jennings was duly condemned and pardoned.   I went to the prison myself, took him to the Legation in a carriage, prevented his speaking to anyone.   The next morning the Military Attaché took him down to Puerto Barrios, sitting beside van Jennings like a guard, permitting him still to speak to no one until he was duly delivered to the captain of an American vessel in the harbor.   In my turn I had promised Estrada that van Jennings would not make trouble in the country after his release and that I would see that he departed by the first ship.   I did.

Another case was that of the local manager of the Guatemala-San José railroad, an American citizen.   He came into my house one evening in great urgency.   It seemed that the railroad and the Government had been in dispute for a considerable period on a matter of taxes ; that the railroad had withheld payment pending a settlement.   The Government had unearthed a law by which non-payment of taxes for a certain period gave grounds for foreclosure unless a bond could be posted that adequately covered any possible assessment.   A friend of the manager had just whispered to him that he was to be served with a summons that night to post a bond of $200,000 in twenty-four hours or the railroad would be seized and sold at auction for taxes.   The night was Thursday, the following day was Good Friday ; Saturday, Easter Sunday and Monday were holidays not only for the banks in Guatemala, but also for those in Boston, the head offices of the railroad.   There was no way of raising such a sum.   The manager was frantic.   There was nothing for it, we had to hide him to prevent the summons being served until Tuesday by which time he could arrange by cable to have the bond posted.   By that time it was midnight, but he must not be found the next morning in the capital, nor could he return to his house that night.   I sallied out to the livery stable, woke up a watchman and got two saddle horses.   I picked up the manager at my house and we rode out to the 'finca' of a mutual friend, while

I got back to town before dawn broke. His wife telephoned the next day that the process servers had arrived late that night ; that she had stated that her husband was not home and she didn't know where he was.   She told the truth — she didn't know and we didn't tell her. The Government won something nevertheless, because the tax matter was settled to their satisfaction on Tuesday.

At one stage of my stay, the Government of the United States had a lively disagreement with Estrada Cabrera and it was thought expedient to send an American naval vessel to San José and for its captain to make an official visit in the capital ; this would add to the scene, it was felt, one of those elements that Bismarck spoke of as 'imponderables.'   The Captain duly arrived, a fine figure of a seaman, ruddy faced and stalwart, with keen blue eyes under heavy brows. We conferred about his call on the President, and since he said he spoke Spanish, we decided that he would address Estrada Cabrera a short declaration in that tongue. So we prepared it.   The Captain then retired to my smoking room to memorize his piece, but though he would report every fifteen minutes that the piece was mastered, when I heard him, he never failed to twist it or to forget it altogether. In desperation, he conceived a brilliant idea, no less than to type it concisely and to paste it inside his cocked hat which, being in uniform, he would carry during the interview. We were shown into the presence of the President, I duly presented the Captain, and he began his speech, his cocked hat on his arm with the text available at a glance. 'Señor Presidente,' he began, and his blue eyes sought the text. 'Tengo el honor,' the eyes sought the text again, and so he read it through. Estrada's little eyes were twinkling, and his lips under the moustache were twitching before the end, but he gravely congratulated the Captain on his Spanish; I fear some of the effect of the 'imponderable' was lost.

The Captain was insistent that, since the trouble of which I spoke was centred in San José, I should accompany him to the coast and be received on the cruiser officially and get the salute which no inhabitant of the town could miss. Frock coated and silk hatted I accompanied him. We lunched on board, and since the rules regarding hospitality in the Navy were not as rigid then as now, we ate and drank abundantly. In the stifling heat, and in the clothes I wore, my collar and shirt were limp. The Captain instructed me in taking the salute. I was to descend into the pinnace which would be pulled to the bow of the cruiser; I was then to stand up, hat in hand, while the salute was fired. All went well until I got up. The pinnace was rising and falling in the huge swell, the gun blazed over my head, and I tumbled ignominiously into the thwarts. I scrambled to my feet, the gun blazed its full eleven shots for a Chargé d'Affaires and I returned completely deafened to San José.

The most troublesome cases were those arising from claims of citizens who were technically American but of dubious allegiance. It seemed as if numerous prospective mothers, Guatemalan, Honduran and others, had taken trips to the United States for the sole purpose of having their children born on our territory and thus escaping, or being furnished with an excuse for escaping, many of the vexations of life with which citizens of the country were harassed. There were several American citizens in Guatemala who spoke no English

and whose last sight of American soil had been the first sight
they had had of any soil.   Several of them were wealthy and
had extensive lands.   On the land, labor problems presented
special features.   All men of military age were subject to call
to the colors.   This law made a harvest for the local governors, 'jefes politicos' they were called.   It was their habit
to call on the large land-owners just before the crops had to be
picked or the coffee beans collected and to present an order
in all gravity summoning the workmen to the army.   The
owner would protest that it was crop time.   The jefe would
then propose that the matter could be adjusted by the payment
of a per capita forfeit in lieu of service.   The owner usually
had to pay.   Although the 'American citizens' felt that they
had been born above these irritations, they would pay the for-
feits to save the crops.   When the harvest was completed they
would ride to the capital, come to see me and demand the head
of the jefe on a charger or at least their money back.

The question of what constituted an American citizen was
always troublesome.   The Guatemalan Government would
admit the Legation's right to protect the native born, as well
as naturalized Americans who were born elsewhere than in
Guatemala.   They would never admit that their own citizens
could alienate their nationality, return to Guatemala and enjoy the status of American citizens.   Of course we tried to
claim that right, and the State Department made repeated attempts to negotiate a treaty by which Guatemala surrendered
its claims.   When my new Minister finally arrived, a clergyman for his first sixty years of life, he was looking over past
business to familiarize himself with the situation.   He came
across a note to the Foreign Office which I had written on this

subject. After reading it he said, 'That is an excellent presentation of the subject. I don't see how they can fail to accept our point of view.' I replied, 'I never would accept it if I were the President of Guatemala.' Surprised and slightly shocked, Dr. Leavell asked, 'Do you mean to say that you sent a note urging them to a course of action which you did not consider beneficial to their country?' 'Dr. Leavell,' I said, 'I don't think I ever thought it through before, but here is my attitude. I may use my best endeavor to persuade my Government to adopt a given course. If I succeed, I naturally do my best to make that course a success. But if my Government insists on a certain course, and I am unable to persuade them that they are wrong, then I am in the same position as an attorney. I either do my best for my principal or, if the course is flagrantly against my conscience, I must resign. But as long as I stay I must use my best ability to carry out what my Government eventually decides is proper.'

I have often thought over this conversation. I believe still that such is the proper attitude of a government representative. His criticism of his Government's attitude may and should be made to his Government, but to nobody else, and once a course is decided upon, he must push it with all his might or get out.

I then went on to explain that if the Guatemalan Government admitted the right of its citizens to become Americans and enjoy the privileges of American citizens on their return to Guatemala, every man of sufficient fortune in the country would take out our citizenship as a guarantee to his property; not only that, he would send his sons to be educated in the United States, to acquire citizenship at the same time. The result would be a privileged property class owing no allegiance to the President and immune from the prevailing methods of carrying on a government. Estrada Cabrera would never admit this change. I do not know whether the situation has been altered subsequently. Perhaps the strictness with which we now apply our laws of nationality in respect to naturalized citizens returning to their country of origin has reassured the Guatemalans, and they now acquiesce in our point of view.

One class of callers at my office was a source of never failing interest to me. Concession hunters had never before swum into my ken, but they were numerous and persistent in Guatemala. They were widely different in appearance, but they had a lot in common. All were immaculately dressed, nearly all wore jewels, whether in stick pins, cuff links or shirt studs, and all gave away excellent cigars. But it was in their conversation that they showed the greatest similarity. They were confident, self-assured. They talked spaciously of millions and cited well-known figures in American finance by first names. They were all convinced of the mighty fortunes to be amassed, and the vast benefits that would accrue to the Guatemalan Government from their projects. They had so hypnotized themselves with the magnificence of their dreams that their hard eyes would glisten as they discoursed on them. They believed in fairies and in Santa Claus, and they nearly made me believe too.

One man, especially, had a conception for a romance. He was after nothing less than the whole province of Petén which lies in the extreme northeasterly section of the country. At that time it was little explored, inhabited only by indigenous Indians who spoke no Spanish, a vast territory, unknown and believed to hide fabulous wealth. Under the plan the Guatemalan Government would have surrendered sovereignty in all except name against a payment of a percentage of the profits. The company would have set up a local administration, built roads, schools, hospitals, all the normal adjuncts of civilization. Gold mines would have been exploited, but it was calculated that teak wood alone would make a nice profit. Steamship lines, river boats, the limitless imagination of the project was dazzling. It was to spring up full-grown — none of your slow growth like the Hudson Bay Company, or the East Indian concessions.

Their visits, the concession hunters themselves, always had the quality of a dream. They would come, they would declaim, they would invite me to dinner. When I had advised them as to whom they should see, they would depart, and I would never see them again, alas. In no single instance did I learn from their lips the fate of their projects.

The biggest diplomatic episode that happened while I was there was not directly connected with the American Legation. The London market had floated a Guatemalan Government loan which was secured by a direct export tax on each bag of coffee. The Guatemalan Government had defaulted for several years when the British Government sent as Minister Sir Lionel Cardon, a red-faced, white-haired, choleric gentleman of great determination and explosive temperament. Negotiations dragged because after all Central America was in the Caribbean region and the special interest of the United States in all that took place had to be considered ; Estrada Cabrera took full advantage of this happy fact. Sir Lionel kept me in touch with negotiations, and at the same time the British Embassy was busy persuading the State Department at Washington that drastic action had to be taken. Finally matters were settled in Washington, Sir Lionel laid down an ultimatum in Guatemala that if the tax was not immediately restored to the service of the loan, the British Legation would depart bag and baggage and the British Government would reserve the right to take such steps as it deemed necessary. A time limit was set for the answer. If it did not arrive by eight o'clock one evening, all bets were off. I rode out to the British Legation that afternoon, luggage was strewn about, the staff were clad in frock coats and polishing silk hats to make the departure of the Legation as impressive as possible. Sir Lionel was striding up and down the hall, red in the face, white moustache bristling, bursting into repeated explosions of wrath and denunciations of Estrada Cabrera. The opposition of the Guatemalans collapsed, but I have always been sorry that I did not witness the silk-hatted departure of a Legation.

CHAPTER V

On the outskirts of the city lies a steep hill, the Cerrito del Carmen. Like all bold positions in Catholic lands, the summit is crowned with a church, one built in the days when churches were fortresses with stout stone buttresses and watch towers. I used to climb there often in the late afternoon and listen to the evening service. The place was lonely, far above the city, and the worshippers were usually restricted to a handful of Indians who had come in for market, climbed the hill and had left their baskets and burdens at the door. After the bright sunlight, the interior was dark, lit by two candles only and the open door. As my eyes became accustomed to the dusk I began to distinguish the comforting colors of old velvet and tapestry and to watch the candle-light wink on old Spanish silver. The incense would reach my nostrils while the priest murmured in Latin, and the black-haired figures in brilliant shawls kneeled silently before him.

Then I would go out and lie on the grass, looking down on the old city. No sound reached the elevation. The city seemed to sleep. The pastel monotony of the streets had vanished. From above, Guatemala was a huge garden cut by wide walls. The walls were the roofs of the houses, the patios the gardens. There was a wealth of trees, and flowers in such mass and color as to be visible from this distance. A far-off tolling of a church bell sounded the hour of evening service. It was taken up and repeated in various tones until the bells of the Cathedral joined the chant, deep and purposeful. At the distance the tones blended harmoniously, a liquid melody calling to prayer. The shadow of the huge cathedral lengthened over the city, while the figures of the worshippers, foreshortened and tiny, crossed the squares for their evening devotion.

I am not a Catholic, but I began to think of the Church. I thought of its vitality and its ability to survive. As an historical monument alone it is unique in western civilization. I was about to couple Roman law with the Church as another example of survival, but it is not fair. Roman law has been distorted and changed ; the Catholic Church has remained what it was. It kept alive the pursuit of classical learning through the Middle Ages, it carried on the tradition of Rome, and enjoyed the prestige of the former Empire. Supple but unchangeable, diplomatic but stubborn, it has lived through the crash of Kingdom, Empire, and Democracy. It remains what it was centuries ago, rebuking the rulers of the world when it appears needful, the only force in the west that is listened to with reverence beyond national frontiers. It is a force with which rulers must reckon, whether they like it or not, whether they believe or not in the Catholic faith. The mightiest of statesmen have been beaten by its persistence.

I thought of the beauty of the Church. The windows at Chartres, the cathedrals at Rheims, at Milan, and elsewhere. Beauty was encouraged by the Church ; through its history the best of architects, painters, glass makers, silversmiths, artisans, all worked for the Church. Even in the remotest villages the people do their loving best to make the church beautiful. Protestant churches and cathedrals in Continental Europe are as if a dead hand had been laid upon them. So many of them have suffered from the ministrations of men who felt in their hearts that there was something incompatible between beauty and reverence. Only in England in some of the great cathedrals of the Church of England has beauty been preserved. And it was preserved and not created. Most of those cathedrals were erected by men of Catholic faith.

I thought of the nearness of the Church to its people, of its extraordinary ability to be all things to all men. It appeals to the peasant and to the man of education ; an appeal by different means, by different facets, but at core the same. The edifice itself is a place to be used. The Indian brings his lunch and eats it in the cool porch of the church. He brings his children and his animals to be blessed. He is married in it, he is buried from it and he stops in it as he passes, to say his prayer. To the intellectual it offers repose from doubt and struggle, the certainty and authority of final decision that render the soul struggle futile. It is all things to all men. The priest in his confessional deals with every class of human error, no son or daughter of the Church but may share his burden and so alleviate it. It takes infinite interest in the daily doings of mankind and so understands him. Because Catholicism can be simple to the simple man, it is the inestimable boon to millions. Fortunate indeed are those who are born in the faith.

The lights had come on in the city, the stars showed palely in the darkening sky, and I came down the Cerrito del Carmen and returned to the capital.

The first few months I was lonely. I never admitted it to myself, but I think now I must have been homesick. Especially during the nights of the rains, when it was nearly impossible to go out, I would listen to the ceaseless beat on the tiles and the splash of the drain pipes into the pila, imagine what my friends were doing at home and long for the evening diversions of a great city. Gradually contentment entered my mind, and I began to realize the great truth that happiness does not depend on externals but arises from a man's own state of mind for which he is himself largely responsible. It was as if I suddenly became free. I knew that theatres, music, the intellectual stimulus of a great city were pleasant accessories of life but no more. I knew that never again would my peace of mind depend on them. A man's ultimate resources are within himself. At some stage of life he must realize this or he is haunted by the fear of loneliness. I would enjoy these diversions again when they came. I would even seek them eagerly, but I would always know that I could do without them.

A small band of us became constant companions. There was my opposite number in the British Legation, in charge as I was for a long period of time. Godfrey Haggard, now Consul-General in Paris, was tall, angular, freckle-faced, crowned with a fiery red head. His speech was eccentric, his humor boisterous and all-embracing. A provocative talker, we spent hours in argument on all conceivable subjects. His wife, Georgiana, was a French Canadian from the Province of Quebec. She talked English with an engaging accent. Delicate in features and appearance, she went on trips with us on horse or on foot and was certainly not the most exhausted at the end. Honest and direct, she had the charm of real simplicity of spirit. Da Costa Carneiro, the Portuguese representative, was another companion with a delightful wife. Da Costa was lean, wore a monocle, was an incessant and humor-

ous talker in a resonant baritone.   With the precocious cyni-
cism of the Latin he loved to deflate the flights of enthusiasm of
Godfrey and myself.   Our conversation was unique as to
language.   Haggard knew Spanish and some French, I just
the opposite, Da Costa knew French and Spanish but very little English.   We never knew exactly which language we were
speaking.   Our local tongue became a mixture of three.   One
day Haggard pointed to a hill in front of us and remarked, 'Il
faut subir esta colina hasta the top.'   It typified our method
of communication.

One scene of the three of us I hold vividly in mind.   We
had determined on a long excursion, something over twenty
miles on foot.   Da Costa presented himself shod for the rocky
path in white canvas tennis shoes.   After the first five miles
they were in ribbons.   So were his feet.   The situation was
serious so we sat down to take counsel.   Presently an Indian
lad appeared leading a diminutive donkey almost obscured by
two wicker baskets lashed to its sides.   We entered into negotiation, found the lad had been to market with vegetables.
Fortunately he had sold them all, and the baskets were empty.
We hired boy and donkey, Da Costa stepped astride just in
front of the baskets.   I can see it now, Haggard and I striding along the dusty path, Da Costa between us on the tiny
beast, talking as ever in his resonant voice.   His monocle
flashed in the sun and his tennis shoes at the end of his long
legs just missed the path.   The Indian lad followed, every
now and then he prodded the donkey with a sharp stick to
make him keep pace with us.   Thus we returned, and thus
we presented ourselves to Mme. Da Costa on her doorstep.

The only carriage road that ran out of the capital led to

Antigua Guatemala.   I call it a carriage road because it could
be traversed in carriage or diligence.   But it was so dusty or so
full of axle-deep mudholes in the rains and so bumpy that we
usually did it on foot or on horseback.   The road wound
around the shoulder of a range of hills that separated the two
cities.   On the summit of the shoulder lay a little inn called
San Rafael, kept by a Spanish landlord with a French wife
from Dijon.   The inn was the customary adobe dwelling, but
it had a little brick terrace edged by giant eucalyptus trees,
with stiff formal beds of pansies and tulips.   On the terrace
at a table spread with a red and white checked cloth, we would
halt for lunch.   Madame would serve a delicious meal, bringing out the courses herself and talking and gesticulating so
eloquently I feared for the dishes.   She talked of her land of
Burgundy, of the food they ate, frogs' legs and escargots, of the
wines they produced, especially of the Mar de Bourgogne.
Poor soul, she had left her land fifteen years before and had
given up hope of seeing it again.

I hesitate to write of Antigua.   It stays in my memory so
gently and beautifully, like a benediction from an ancient and
reverent holy man.   I notice that Addison Mizner in *Many
Mizners* talks of the city with a reverence that he shows for few
other things.   It lies in a lovely valley at the foot of the Vol-
cano Agua, sloping symmetrically like Fujiyama and towering
to a lovely cone of snow in the winter.   The city was the
Captaincy-General of Central America for considerably
longer than the United States has existed.   The great earthquake which destroyed it did so gracefully.   It left façades
of baroque graciousness.   It left lovely interiors of churches
with wide gaps in the roof through which the sun pours on

painted walls. Services continue in the half-ruined edifices. Where gentlemen in lace and armor received the benediction, groups of patient Indians take the same sacrament. Winding in and out and among the ruins, lines of coffee trees glisten in the sun, their red berries standing out like decorations on a Christmas tree. The place was a market for ecclesiastic things of beauty. I used to bring travelling Americans over to see it. If they were women they fell into a passion of bargaining. In those days I had no acquisitive sense; indeed, throughout my life things have meant very little. I rejoice as well as any other in a gracious existence but can leave one set of surroundings and enter another with complete ease and comfort. So I acquired none of these things in Antigua and enjoyed only vicariously the passion of shopping and bargaining.

I made numerous trips. Travel took little preparation and next to no expense. The inns in the villages were primitive — cell-like rooms with a bed and chair, tiled floor, no ventilation save the door itself. Fleas and other insects were prevalent, so it was well to travel with a hammock which could be strung out of reach of all but the most active. Bread, too, was a good thing to take along ; otherwise, you lived on 'frijole' beans, and chicken. For butter, the meat of the aguacate, or alligator pear, made a good substitute. Coffee naturally could be had anywhere. The natives roasted the bean, ground it to dust, let cold water drip slowly through it, catching the black liquid in a pan below. This liquid, an essence of coffee of staggering strength, was served cold in a carafe. You poured it into your cup and added boiling water or milk somewhat as you mix a whisky and soda and in about the same proportions.

We planned a trip once to Lake Atitlán, the scene of one of Alvarado's most important battles. There were Haggard and his wife, Miss Owen, an American girl living in Guatemala, and myself. We were to take the train to San José on the Pacific, thence north by train towards the Mexican frontier, the final section of the voyage on foot. The government heard of our intention so when we reached the station in the morning we found a private car attached at our disposal. We were delighted and made ourselves comfortable. At the first station we heard shouts, followed by a blare of music, rushed to the back platform and found the dignitaries of the city, the local band and the station draped in all the American and British flags and their approximation that could be scraped together. The Mayor made a speech, Haggard and I replied, warm champagne was brought and drunk, and the train pulled out twenty-five minutes late. At the next station — same performance and train forty minutes late. By this time Godfrey and I decided that conservation was necessary both of voice and liquor capacity, so at succeeding stations we alternated, one doing the honors while the other hid and rested. This went on all day, and it was quite a day.

Atitlán was a jewel of a lake. I understand you can motor there now over a respectable road, and that hundreds and thousands of tourists make the trip in ease. But when we went the Quiché Indians lived in their villages exactly as they did when Alvarado came. They spoke the same tongue, and if you can judge from old pictures, wore the same clothes. They certainly seemed as curious and interested in seeing white people as they would have been had we been discoverers of the land. They were patient, friendly people, dignified and of painstaking courtesy. I had no feeling we were running any risk among them. I never carried a weapon beyond a stout stick in case the village dogs got ugly. On our return we were spending the night at Pacayál, a coffee finca belonging to Mr. Hodgsdon, an American. It was a lovely spot with a view of the Pacific slope that was breath-taking. It was here that I got the only real SOS that Palma sent me from the Legation. He telegraphed the code word that meant 'Gallop all the way.' Mr. Hodgsdon rose to the occasion. He sent me off in the morning at dawn on a sweet-gaited mare that went up hill and down dale at the same agreeable little pace. An Indian followed on a mule, leading another in case my mare became exhausted. I changed two or three times to rest her, but she never showed signs of wear. I reached Antigua about 6 p.m., hired a diligence and four horses and made the return to the capital at a gallop over the bumps. The mare would have been much better. Never have I been so battered. What was worse was that the urgent affair for which I had been summoned had already settled itself.

I often went to the banana lands. Growing bananas was a curious industry. The way they did it, at least in Guatemala, was simple. Little was contributed by man ; most was done by nature. The low heavily wooded plains near the Motagua River make splendid banana country. First they cut the jungle ; it isn't necessary to clear it of rubbish, for wood and refuse rot with amazing rapidity in the damp heat. Planting consists in merely shoving shoots into the soft earth. In the first year after the jungle has been felled, banana trees push up through stumps and rotting logs. By the end of a couple of years all trace of the jungle has disappeared. When the bananas are ripe the tree is ten to a dozen feet high. Bunches are not plucked as with most fruit ; rather the tree itself is plucked. A negro cuts through the soft stalk with one sweep of his heavy machete ; as the tree falls it is caught in a forked stick to prevent the fruit from hitting the ground and being bruised. The bunch is then held, severed and laid gently on a small wagon on temporary rails that have been laid along the line of the day's cutting. Bananas for distant markets are not yellow when gathered. They are cut still green and ripen during the voyage and marketing. They are so perishable that most careful calculations are made of the time elapsing between the cutting and the supposed market in order to have them reach the point of sale in prime condition. When they are allowed to ripen on the tree and are eaten fresh, they have a pungent flavor that they lose in distant voyages ; they are as superior to the ordinary banana of the market as the pineapple ripened on the bush and eaten fresh is superior to the market article.

In the midst of the banana fields of the United Fruit Company one great stretch of forest remains intact. In its midst, in the same surroundings in which they have lain for centuries, are the Mayan ruins of Quiriguá. Sylvanus Morley was in charge of the excavations. It was fascinating to visit him and have him tell of the meaning and possibilities of the study of this ancient civilization. Since then extensive Mayan ruins have been uncovered elsewhere, especially in Yucatán, but I believe then that those of Quiriguá were the most famous. Happily, the stretch of forest which sheltered Quiriguá was the most stately and beautiful jungle I have ever seen. The comparison of the jungle to a cathedral has become trite, yet it is the inevitable thought that strikes the man who enters. The same soft greenish light, the same rare shafts of sunlight piercing a semi-obscurity, the same mighty columns meeting in vaulted Gothic arches high above. The same stillness prevails. It is wrong to think of the jungle as full of noise of animals and birds. On the edge of a forest one hears parrots, monkeys and a thousand other living things. But these creatures live, so to speak, on the roof of the cathedral ; within its depths the silence is absolute as if the cathedral were on a desert island and the worshipper were alone in his prayers.

One afternoon I arrived at Virginia, the headquarters of the Fruit Company. Victor Cutter met me at the train as we were to push on at once to Puerto Barrios, there to meet a steamer early the next morning which was bringing my brother Oliver and his friend Will Dunham on a visit. Three negroes loaded a hand-car onto the track. Cutter and I sat on the front bench with our guns, and the negroes set the gasoline engine in movement. The noise of the motor awakened every creature of the jungle that bordered the tracks with two dense green walls. Parrots squawked, macaws screamed, monkeys chattered. Birds of every color sailed over us. Suddenly a great black turkey-cock soared across the track. Simultaneously we raised our guns and fired. The turkey dropped on the track so close the negroes nearly threw us out of the car by the violence with which they jammed on the brake. He was a beautiful bird, yellow head and crest, copper black in the body with a sheen of deep green on the wing. A little farther along another turkey sailed into sight. I raised my gun, but Cutter hissed savagely, 'Don't shoot.' He explained in whispers, 'Didn't you see those niggers' eyes bulge at the first shot ?

They never before saw anyone hit a bird on the wing when moving along a railroad. We would probably miss the second shot and spoil the whole thing.' I didn't fire another shot from the car, and our prestige was saved.

Rolling along on the flat-car, Cutter proposed, and I enthusiastically assented, that we take Oliver and Will straight off the boat into the swamps on an expedition after wild pigs. It was dreadful country, Cutter explained, and if we took them there straight from the boat it would give them an impression that they would talk about the rest of their lives. We boarded the ship before daylight in a thunderstorm of tropic violence, took them off to breakfast in Puerto Barrios, rushed them into old clothes, put guns in their hands and departed again in the flat-car. The thunder had ceased, but drizzle continued and dawn broke on as dreary a scene as I ever witnessed. We left the car and began our hunt. No meditations on the majesty of the jungle haunted me that day. We waded through water usually half way up the calf of the leg, we slipped in mud. We fell against trees with jagged bark that tore our hands painfully. Cutter said they were called 'Jesus Christ trees' at the moment ; they always bore the name applied to them by the last unfortunate that fell against them. We were so miserable that we never stopped for lunch but pushed on until about four when we came upon a slight elevation, perhaps a foot above standing water. There the negroes prepared our hammocks, each one in a little house of palm trees and each covered with its mosquito net. We were so dead tired we crawled into the hammocks before darkness was complete and slept like logs except when a hole in the roof let through a stream of water that had to be plugged. When I woke the next morning the net was covered with slimy, crawling things. I lit a cigar before I got up to blow them away. The same story the next day on our return. The closest we came to the pigs was to smell some and it is like no other smell.

CHAPTER VI

Social life was diverting. The rigid formalism of Spanish civilization was pressed upon a laughter-loving, quick-tempered people. Usually the formalism was maintained, occasionally the instincts of the people burst through, a scene of heated realism took place, then the formalism was resumed. It was rare that a young man was invited into a girl's house. As a rule he stood on the sidewalk outside her window, while she sat on the window seat within and gossiped through stout iron bars. He was a bold young man, at any rate, if he accepted an invitation to enter. The family would gradually and unostentatiously slip away, the man would discover himself alone with the lady who was thereby compromised. His intentions had better be honorable ! But the girls were given a large measure of liberty provided the liberty did not involve being alone with a man. Dances were popular, often in the ball-rooms of the clubs, sometimes on pavilions erected outside the houses during fiesta seasons, more rarely in private houses where we danced on the tiled terraces that surround the patio. Orchestras performed in the clubs, but for outdoors and private houses it was simpler to bring in a 'marimba.' This instrument has become known abroad in recent years. It is a sort of over-sized xylophone with metal keys played by four men armed with little hammers. Young men and girls could ride and drive together, always in bands. They could even go to the cinema but, by some curious taboo, not to the play or opera. The first year I bought a box for the opera season, but when I had used it a couple of times I was ready to surrender it to any enthusiast who could live through the dullness of the performances. It was quite a job giving the tickets away. I would send out a messenger with a list of half a dozen people who I thought might accept. By the time the messenger got back a couple of other messengers had arrived at my house offering me somebody else's tickets. Since it was frowned upon to leave your box empty, its disposal shortened my life.

The American Club was the centre of much of the gaiety. It had a large ball-room, a large billiard room, and a larger bar. The gentlemen of the capital loved the game of billiards. They would take off their white coats to play, and as they stretched over the table to make a shot, the outline of revolvers in the hip-pocket deformed the contour of their breeches. The biggest event of the year was the 4th of July ball at the Club. It began each time very formally. The guests were received by the President of the Club and myself with proper deference to protocol. But after a couple of hours of roaring trade at the bar, a good time was had by all. Rosita came to the ball escorted by a Costa Rican gentleman of ancient lineage and choleric disposition, extremely enamored of Rosita. She looked like a fairy-tale princess, small and slight, tiny hands and feet, great black eyes, wavy black hair and a smile that could make the heart of any man give a sudden lurch and resume its beat at accelerated pace. Rosita spoke four languages, and when angered by the presumption of one of her partners, her flow of invective in all four tongues would have brought a blush of shame to the cheek of the most fluent of mule drivers. Her dancing was like her appearance, dainty, effortless and vitally alive. An American from the Fruit Company banana lands was attending the 4th of July ball like a good American citizen. Also like a good American citizen, he was standing in a group of stags taking little part in the dancing. Suddenly he and Rosita saw each other, a *coup de foudre!* From then on they were never separated. What made it the more agonizing to the Costa Rican escort was the fact that the American was a spirited dancer and was teaching Rosita strange things called 'bunny-hug' and 'fox-trot' — dances which he had just imported from the United States. We had never seen them in Guatemala. They were slightly shocking, and Rosita took to them like a duck to water. Late in the evening Rosita came to me decorously with the American to say good night. I inquired after the Costa Rican, who was glowering from across the room. Rosita said with simple candor, 'I don't like him any more ; Dr. Duncan is taking me home.' From this point I ceased to be an eye-witness of events, and must report by hearsay. As Rosita and the Doctor left the Club entrance the Costa Rican came charging toward them, gun in hand. Someone cried a warning, and man and girl dashed down the street pursued by the Costa Rican. They turned the corner. The Costa Rican reached it and fired. Rosita fell, shot through the thigh, but struggled to her knees and tackled the Costa Rican as he went by, tripped and held him until some guests from the dance came on the run and disarmed him. The American, I regret to say, disappeared around the next corner, ran to his hotel, hastily packed a bag and departed for the banana lands by the next train. The city went wild over Rosita. Poets wrote verses to her, flowers filled her room to bursting. Everybody called, and Rosita received us in bed. Dressed in lace, surrounded by flowers, her wavy hair on the pillow, her great eyes filled with tears, she deplored the notoriety she had won.

Victor Cutter told me a sequel to the tale. It appears that the Costa Rican was arrested but shortly released on a promise to leave the country. Apparently the Court had viewed with sympathy the torture of jealousy through which he had passed and had not desired to prosecute. The Costa Rican took the train for Puerto Barrios and the news of his coming reached the banana lands before him. The American breathed dire threats of what he would do to the Costa Rican when he caught him on the train, so Cutter was present when the train pulled in. The American swung on board before it stopped and proceeded through the coaches hunting his victim. The latter was discovered leaning over the rail of the back platform contemplating the scenery. As he leaned, the butt of his pistol showed above his hip-pocket. The American turned to Cutter who was watching breathless with excitement and said in a resigned voice, 'Oh Lord, I guess it isn't worth while' ; then left the train.

The ball was not the only episode of the 4th of July. During the afternoon I held a reception. Diplomats would come, Guatemalans would come, American citizens would come, as well as all who had even a remote claim to citizenship. I remember once a group of three black negroes, dressed in shining white, presented themselves. Da Costa, my Portuguese friend, murmured to me, 'Voici que les negatives photographiques présentent leurs hommages.' The negroes assured me that they were born in New Orleans but had lost their

papers. Their manner of speech was pure Elizabethan. I
knew that no such purity of archaic English sprang from our
soil. Subsequently I mentioned the visit to Haggard who
recognized my description and identified them as Jamaican
negroes who had found Haggard and the British Legation unwilling to press their claim on the government and who had
then told him that they would become American citizens and
get justice. The guests consumed enormous quantities of
champagne and cigars ; I used to import a special 4th of July
cigar from Jamaica — they disappeared by the box ! The
high spot of the afternoon was the arrival of a 'floral tribute,'
it merited the grandiloquent phrase, from the President of the
Republic. An officer on horseback with drawn sword would
clatter over the flagstones, followed by four bare-footed soldiers staggering under an enormous basket of flowers eight feet
high and crowned with a huge bow of red, white, and blue
ribbon. The officer would enter the salon, the soldiers would
plant the basket in the middle of the floor and wipe the sweat
from their eyes, the officer would salute with drawn sword and
make a speech. I would reply, everybody would down a
glass of champagne and everybody would cheer.

Guatemalan society went in a body to the races, pouring
out the Reforma drive in all manner of vehicles and afoot.
Cash prizes were posted, and were deductible from the gate
receipts. Another deduction had been sanctioned by custom,
champagne for the judges, who could be recognized as such
by their top hats. There was always some uneasiness among
horse owners in the last races lest the gate receipts should be
exhausted and the cash prizes in forfeit. The largest owner
was one Schurman, incidentally the proprietor of the livery

stable.   He usually had two or more entries for each race and apparently made a good thing of it.   One day, just before the last race, he was seen running at top speed to the paddock, crying out to his agent at the top of his lungs, 'Cancel my horses for this race, no more money for prizes, the judges are drinking beer.'   Among the judges was an Englishman, Edward Bellingham, who stood out like a rock against the casual rulings of the local judges.   He rigidly upheld the best traditions of the British turf.

Bellingham had been an officer in the South African war and had served with distinction.   His knowledge of Spanish was remarkable and he was working in the British Legation as a sort of attaché-interpreter.   On week-ends he went prospecting among the hills but I fear with little result.   I lost sight of him for years, but in 1920 I attended a ball given by Lady D'Abernon in the British Embassy at Berlin.   I was making my way through the press around the bar when I bumped someone violently, turned to say I was sorry, and found myself faced by Bellingham.   He was wearing the uniform of a Colonel, his breast blazed with ribbons, among them the D.S.O.   While we consumed a whisky and soda he told me his story.   At the outbreak of the war he had hurried back to England and re-entered the Army.   By one of those whirligigs of fortune with which every reader of British fiction is familiar, an uncle had died and he was Sir Edward Bellingham, Baronet, and master of an ample fortune.   He was in Berlin as a member of the British section of the Commission of Control and was about to retire to enjoy his inheritance.   Other officers told me that Bellingham had been an extraordinary soldier, that his personal bravery was remarkable and that his men would follow him anywhere.

I have already mentioned Baron von Merck, the aide-de-camp to President Estrada Cabrera.   I never knew his reason for coming to Guatemala.   On my arrival he had already been there a number of years and always in the President's employ. He was a stalwart, red-faced individual with tremendous, almost frightening, gales of laughter and sudden demoniac attacks of rage.   Money ran through his fingers like water both to satisfy his whims and thorough generosity.   He was like a great overgrown boy but more dangerous.   Estrada Cabrera knew him thoroughly so did not pay him a salary.   He gave him a house, next door to mine, and from time to time sums of money which usually lasted about three days.   Von Merck loved to give parties and would urge me to come.   My taste was not fastidious in those days but occasionally I would wish I had declined.   So I hit on a device which proved useful. When I was invited to one of his parties, I would wait in my house until I heard the marimba and knew the party had started, then climb a ladder to the top of the wall which separated our two patios, look over his party and decide on my attendance.

Once he banged on my door and asked me to come to his house.   Bellingham was there, and they were discussing a grave matter on which Von Merck wanted my advice.   I joined the consultation and heard the problem.   It seems that Bellingham had some furniture he was selling for someone, and Von Merck was anxious to purchase it.   The problem was bald in its simplicity ; Von Merck as usual had no money —

how to get it out of the President? Several solutions were proposed, discussed, and rejected. At last Von Merck shouted, 'I've got it. Bellingham, you write me a letter saying that you have sold me the furniture and abusing me for not paying the bill. If the letter is sufficiently scurrilous, I can take it to the President and say that for the dignity of his household, and to prevent an unpleasant incident with a foreigner, he must let me have the money.' He and Bellingham sat at the desk and, both masters of Spanish, composed a letter of such studied insult that Von Merck was delighted. He carried it off to the President, got his money, and the furniture changed hands.

A group of Spanish and Mexican bull-fighters with all their paraphernalia, including the famous brand of 'Piedras Negras' bulls, visited Guatemala once a year for a brief season. Their visit had the same effect on the city that the visit of the Metropolitan Opera Company would have on a town which had listened to the church choir through long months. The stands were always packed with a crowd as enthusiastic as in Madrid but somewhat less discriminating. Bull-fights in small towns were more amusing. On the days of fiestas a ring was roped off in the village square into which they drove a heifer, her forehead covered with little bunches of gardenias. The lads of the village jumped into the ring one by one and endeavored to pluck out a flower for their girls. The animal had been irritated before the show, and the yells of the crowd stimulated her further, so she always gave the boys a lively chase, sometimes breaking the ropes and scattering the crowd in a frightened flurry of squealing figures. I once saw a lad badly gored ; it was a wonder there weren't more casualties.

The picture of a scene in a bull-fight in the capital stays with me, and a feeling of embarrassment still rises as I think of it. Addison Mizner was visiting Guatemala and sent me a ticket for a box seat for the next day's performance, asking me to join him there. My host was not present on my arrival, and I found myself alone in the great box that faces the entrance, the most prominent position in the stadium. A couple of bulls had been killed, and during the pause which followed, I heard a commotion behind me and turning saw Mizner descending the stairs, a huge figure in ample white flannels, a sombrero hat, pink shirt with mauve tie. On his arm was the largest, pinkest, blondest, most obvious and flamboyant girlfriend I had ever laid eyes on. Every face in the audience turned towards us. I knew what it meant to be the 'cynosure of neighboring eyes.' I thought the ceremony of my presentation to her would never end and that we would never get her seated and her strident voice silenced. Indeed she blazed with more resplendent publicity seated than standing, her conversation was animated, her ostrich plumes nodded and rustled, and her comments on surrounding people were carried on loudly in the complete certainty that none of these people could understand English. She squealed with excitement as the men with the 'capas' dodged the bull's horns by a hair's breadth and applauded enthusiastically when one of them was driven to dive over the barrier into safety. Then came the stage of the 'picadores' who came into the arena mounted on ancient horses and armed with long pikes to hold off the bull's attack. A horse was gored, the spectacle was shocking. The lady gasped and hid her face on Mizner's shoulder, crying out, 'Addison, I can't stand it.' 'It's all right, dearie,' said Mizner,

'I have come prepared.' So saying he pulled an enormous flask from his hip. The lady seized it, tipped back her golden head, raised the flask and the liquor gurgled to its destination. She immediately recovered but had to be repeatedly revived during the subsequent events.

Perhaps I have given the impression that my recollections of the people of Guatemala are all comedy. This is not the case, but the side of their character that gained my affection is much harder to describe. Their hospitality was spontaneous and personal. Their stately courtesy was flavored with the capacity of children for enjoyment. They were unspoiled socially and rejoiced in entertainment that would have bored profoundly a more sophisticated group. Perhaps their interests were insular, nevertheless they were saturated with history, folk-lore and poetry of their region and language. The centre of the world has slipped in the last three hundred years from Madrid and the Spanish orbit ; the people of Guatemala blandly ignored this fact of history. There was something of a past age about them, something reminiscent of the Captaincy-General and the long centuries of dream-like existence remote from the world. I only hope that this flavor has not been destroyed by rapid air service.

The land is new, geologically speaking. Active volcanos are numerous and earthquakes frequent. I gained a sort of technique for earthquakes, learned to jump for the door-frame in case the ceiling fell, to make for the patio and out-of-doors if such was available. You should never run out-doors, however, without a pillow over your head to protect it from tiles which may be shaken loose and fall from the roof. One

night I was in bed when a violent vertical shock set everything trembling. I made for the patio as usual expecting to return to bed in a few minutes when the after tremors had
ceased. But they didn't. They kept on rocking for hours
and I became more and more bored. Electric lights would
not work, nor the telephone ; the city had turned off the current to diminish the risk of fire. I put on some clothes by the
light of the stars and started for the British Legation at the
other end of town. The streets were a sight ; the people had
pulled out sofas, cots, beds, easy chairs. They stuck torches
of resinous wood in the cracks of the flagstones and passed the
hours in accordance with their individual tastes. Some played
the guitar and sang, some made love, some were on their knees
praying that the danger be averted. I found Haggard and
his wife in the garden of the Legation. We decided that the
night should be passed as comfortably as possible. Georgiana
brought the baby into the garden where he slept in his pram.
We brought out a table and chairs, hung a couple of Chinese
lanterns on a tree and played three-handed bridge until daylight. We found the next day that the neighboring town of
Cuajinicalapa had been destroyed. If you pronounce the
word aloud it sounds like an earthquake. It was the most terrific series of shocks that I experienced until Tokyo in 1923.
But that's another story.

I had been in charge nearly two years, Mr. Wilson had become President and Mr. Bryan Secretary of State. I wanted
to get back and see what the Department of State looked like
under the new regime. Besides I had personal reasons for returning. So I rather welcomed the arrival of my new Minis-

ter, Dr. Leavell, and his family and set to work to make them as comfortable as possible, as independent as possible, as quickly as possible. But it wasn't easy. It was my first experience of a non-Service Chief and I was startled by the difficulties with which he was faced. He was a Presbyterian clergyman of magnificent appearance, a face a sculptor would have delighted to model and abundant snow-white hair. He spoke beautiful English, but said himself that he had been too busy mastering that tongue to attempt foreign ones in his lifetime. Mrs. Leavell was lovable, she cooked southern dishes like a master, and she had a sense of humor. They were rigid prohibitionists and served no liquor at the table. Their dinners were either very solemn, or else the diplomats, warned of their views, had taken more than adequate precautions in advance. In the latter event, the dinner went with a rush as far as the salad, and after that collapsed. I had to lead the family around, give lectures like a Dutch uncle but without his authority, from below up, so to speak. I had to translate to the cook, install them in their house and rush around in case of domestic emergency. I didn't like it, and the fact that I had run the show for two years made it the less palatable, and made me the more eager to leave. So I went to Dr. Leavell and asked for permission to request leave of absence. He was most flattering but determined I was not to go ; he needed me. I was obliged to play my last card. I said, 'Would you let me go if I told you I wanted to ask a girl to marry me ?' 'Do you ?' said he. 'Yes,' said I. 'All right,' said Dr. Leavell, and I could have hugged him.

My train pulled out at dawn. On the outskirts of the town I could just make out Haggard waving a sheet from the roof of his house. The sun rose on the steeply sloped hillsides and grew hotter and hotter as we slid into the lowlands. Cutter put me on the boat, and I said good-bye. I left a bit of myself behind.

CHAPTER VII

I landed in New Orleans during Mardi Gras in 1914, hunted up a man I had known in Guatemala, and had an hilarious couple of days. No one who has not spent long periods in remote parts of the world can appreciate the zest for life with which I returned not only to my own country and friends, but to the bewildering enjoyments of a great city. I felt like an explorer in a new land. All sorts of impressions were vividly registered on the sensitive plate which my long absence had caused me to bring to the Carnival of New Orleans. The crowds stimulated me, the beauty of the women excited me, the hearing of my own tongue on all sides made me peculiarly a part of this city bent on amusement. I felt a certain apprehension of the streets, and the rush of motors made me feel like a country cousin marooned on a traffic island at 57th Street and Fifth Avenue. But the very apprehension was stimulating.

Fred Ackert, a boyhood friend of discriminating and even meticulous interest in clothing, was waiting on the platform as the train pulled into Chicago. He took one horrified look at my costume, asked pertinent and searching questions about my wardrobe and hurried me off to a tailor's where he took charge and ordered me a complete new outfit. 'Now,' said Fred, 'we are going to a dance at the Blackstone.'

'But it's only four o'clock in the afternoon,' I objected.

'You don't know the United States ; come and have a look,'

said Fred with an air of tolerant amusement.   It was worth it !
The ball-room was crowded, the blare of noise deafening.   My
first impression was of the advanced age of the dancers.   Soon
I began to recognize mothers and fathers of my friends and a
few friends themselves.   They were doing steps and assuming attitudes that made my eyes bulge.   The city, and the
country, Fred added, had gone dancing mad.   Youth danced
in the evening when work was over ; old age began dancing
in the afternoon.   They all danced and talked dancing, they
danced while they ate, they took lessons in dancing during the
earlier part of the day.   To me, fresh from a simple land, it
seemed Bedlam.   I hated the music and have hated it ever
since.   The dance itself seemed grotesque, grace had departed
as well as that form and those manners without which dancing
ceases to be a diversion of civilized beings.

Unhappily it is not only in dancing that form and manners
have departed.   In writing this observation I am well aware
that by so doing I date myself.   However, the year of my
birth, 1885, is not sufficient indication of my feelings on the
subject.   The date should be pushed much further back, even
to the 18th century, if it is to represent the anachronism which
my mentality presents on the subject of manners.   I have
frequently heard the sturdy and bluff of all nations speak with
contempt of a man of good manners, comparing their own
honesty with the other's insincerity.   As if there were something incompatible between manners and sincerity.   In Heav-
en's name, why can't a man have both ?   Manners ease the
ordinary day-by-day contacts between man and man, between
men and women.   If we are to believe the behaviorists, good
manners should even improve the character.   The constant

act of showing a friendly interest and a kindly consideration of one's fellows should, through its very repetition, create in a man these same characteristics. Manners are not a thing to be put on for formal occasions. They should be an instinctive part of one's make-up and be as evident to a man's wife as to his dinner partner. If a choice between sincerity and manners were necessary, I should unhesitatingly choose manners for 99 per cent. of the people with whom I come in contact and sincerity for the 1 per cent. who were really friends or whom I had to trust in business. But even the 1 per cent. would be better friends and better business men with manners. Good manners are no more indicative of insincerity than bluffness is indicative of honesty. Some of the greatest rogues I have known have earned the adjectives 'bluff,' 'hearty' and 'jovial.'

Years after the time of which I write I was visited in my office in Tokyo by a Japanese gentleman, a great Japanese gentleman as I think this story will prove. The disastrous earthquake and fire of 1923 had just overwhelmed the district, and my friend inquired as to my losses. I told him at some length, feeling rather sorry for myself, that my house had been burned and that we had lost all our possessions. He was duly sympathetic. I inquired as to his experiences. His house, he said with a smile, had been destroyed but he had managed to save certain keepsakes, so it might have been worse. 'And your family ?' I asked. He answered with the smile still bright, 'My daughter was killed.' The sudden lump in my throat nearly choked me, but due to his example I merely said very simply how sorry I was. Good manners on the part of this gentleman had saved us both a deeply painful scene which his instinctive courtesy had wished to spare me. Was such an act an evidence of insincerity ?

This was the second visit I had made to Chicago after a considerable absence. For the first time I began to note consciously the vitality of its people and the rapidity of change not only in the physical appearance of the city, but in customs and way of life. I am tempted to write of Chicago as I have seen it during brief but intimate glimpses at intervals of perhaps two years during a quarter of a century. But Margaret Ayer Barnes has written of all this so competently that any further attempt would be supererogation. *Within This Present* is a sort of compact *Forsyte Saga* of my city, and the various changing scenes of her Chicago family materialize for me the impressions of my brief periodic glimpses. I shortly left for Washington.

Reynolds and Edith Hitt had built a house near Dupont Circle and invited me to stay with them. I was happy that I accepted, for not only was it a pleasure to see them again, but I entered for the first time into Washington life. I first made the acquaintance of numerous people who later became friends. Everybody speaks wistfully of pre-war Washington, and I find myself thinking in the same vein. It was a great village and full of charm. There was little business, no industry, people lived spaciously and took time for leisure. The trees and foliage were so abundant, the streets were so clean and peaceful that one gave little thought to the glaring discrepancies between beautiful buildings and negro hovels. I hate to compare this memory with Washington as I see it now. We have built mightily and beautifully, but to what avail when magnificent buildings are surrounded by an unbroken row of parked cars, tin cans touching heel to toe ?   The row of cars blisters in the heat of summer or shows the unmelted snow of the last winter night.   They are packed so close and remain so permanently that the streets cannot be cleaned. The spotless city has become a place where on a breezy summer day you are choked by little whirlwinds of dust carrying before them Sunday supplements and old rags.   I love the town and hope to live there.   Perhaps by the time I do so some answer to this question of what to do with superfluous Fords may have been found.

The traditional and historic calm of the State Department had been shattered, never to return.   Mr. Bryan sat at Mr. Knox's desk, innumerable callers chatted in the ante-rooms, newspaper correspondents were everywhere, not a single cutaway coat was in evidence.   In the Divisions I found some familiar faces, and one of my friends told me that I should call on the Secretary of State.   I presented myself and waited and waited in the ante-room, looking over the portraits of former Secretaries of State, watched Mr. Bryan burst out of his office, rush to one of the waiting chatting figures and drag him into his office.   At last he rushed out of his door, seized me by the hand and asked my name.   I told him.   He asked where I came from.   I told him.   'Good,' said the Secretary.   'Come and chat with me sometime.'   That was my only interview with the Great Commoner.   It seems to be the fashion to belittle Mr. Bryan, and indeed his methods were not orthodox. But as the years go by, the integrity of his character and the purity of his motives become ever clearer through the revelations of his associates.   Even in achievement he continues to grow ; it is more than probable that his peace treaties will give him a place of significance in the endeavor to replace the decision of the sword with the adjudication of reason and justice. The intimate story of his resignation as Secretary of State shows the drama of an honest man in that most difficult of all dilemmas, a struggle between his conscience on the one hand and his loyalty and expediency on the other.

I modestly inquired in the Latin American Division whether I was to return to Guatemala or be sent elsewhere at the expiration of my leave. Nobody seemed to care particularly or even to be interested, so I offered to go to Europe for a couple of months and relieve them of the burden of making a decision. The proposal appeared acceptable to the others and especially so to me. I tried to see Mr. Wilson in the White House but couldn't pass the Secretary's office, to my great regret, as I had already conceived a deep admiration for the President for the remarkable way in which he had induced Congress to carry out legislation in fulfillment of his election pledges during his brief time in office. In spite of the fact that in succeeding years I was often in correspondence with him, and was in Paris repeatedly during the Peace Conference, I never met or even saw Mr. Wilson. I wish that I had.

Hugh Gibson was on the old steamer *St. Louis* in which we sailed for France, and a more entertaining companion could not be imagined. I had met Hugh before, but I think our friendship dates from that trip. It was a terrible voyage, a continuous storm more violent than anything I have seen on the Atlantic. Passengers were few anyway and still fewer because of the weather, so we were thrown constantly together. We used to sit in the deepest chairs we could find in the deserted smoking room, clinging to the arms to prevent be-

ing thrown out, and talk interminably.   I remember Hugh told
me that he had been through a revolution in Honduras, had
been battered by a paving stone wielded by an ardent anti-
American in Cuba, and now intended to put his feet on his
desk in Brussels where nothing ever happened, light one large
cigar after another, and watch the world roll by.   That was
March 1914.   In five months the German Army rolled by.
We talked often of Latin America and of the curious effects of
Spanish civilization upon Indians and negroes.   Hugh said he
went to a public meeting in the streets of Havana.   Orators
mounted the barrel one after another and harangued the
crowd.   A huge negro climbed on to the stump and began
with these words, 'Nosotros de la raza latina . . .'

Hugh and I have been closely associated in work and play
for years.   An incessant talker, he is never dull, and his observations in the dryest business are lit by flashes of humor.
He writes easily, and his letters are as full of comedy as the
spoken word.   With him the study of the most boring problem becomes a joyous occasion.   The similarity of our names
has caused confusion for years.   After my marriage Hugh
told me he was pursued for months by congratulations and
wedding presents ; the first he returned, the second he kept.
Hugh's personality coupled with real intelligence has made
him one of our outstanding diplomatic officers.   He has been
repeatedly thrust into positions of great responsibility and
has handled them invariably competently and invariably pic-
turesquely.

Katherine Bogle had been living in Paris studying singing
with Jean de Reszke and Arthur Alexander.   Two days after
my arrival Kate agreed to marry me.   There seemed no

point in going home and wasting my leave on preparations
for a formal marriage, so I set about to find what could be done
on the spot in respect to matrimony.   I discovered that marriage in France was a status practically impossible to achieve ;
possibly there is an exception in favor of French citizens.
They demanded birth certificates ; what American ever had
one before the war ?   They demanded parents' consent ; both
mine were dead, and that fact would have to be duly attested.
So I went to London and took counsel with Frank and Helen
Dodge, established my domicile in their house by leaving a
suit-case with some linen in it, arranged to have the banns published in St. Peter's, Eaton Square, and returned to Paris.   The
Arthur Alexanders accompanied us back.   Arthur arranged
the musical program in St. Peter's.   A cousin of mine, Luke
Wilson, arrived, Ned Bell came from the Embassy, Frank and
Helen gave us breakfast, and on April 25th we were married.

Here is the place to jump a bit ahead of my story and tell
about my wife's white dog Kiki.   Kate fell in love with him
at sight in Paris, and he was beautiful when he had just been
washed with bluing.   I duly bought him, but as we left him
in Paris and only picked him up on our return en route to Villa
d'Este, we hadn't really made his acquaintance, nor had I ever
had anything to do with a French Pomeranian, a Lu-Lu they
called it.   That animal's beauty was certainly only skin-deep.
He was a demon by choice, he had the temperament of a
spoiled child, and he had a shrill yap that made you want to
wring his neck.   In New York Kate's sister Winifred came
to our hotel.   Kiki retired under the sofa yapping and only
emerged to bite Win on the ankles.   Win remarked with justi-
fiable acidity, 'Kate, you arrive in New York with your dresses

too tight to step and with a little white dog on the lead. You look like somebody's cutie.' In Chicago he bit my little nephew who tried to play with him. He also assaulted the postman trying to deliver letters to the house. In Glen View he attacked the chauffeur and bit him in the leg. I rushed up with horrid thoughts of damages for hydrophobia, but the chauffeur merely cuffed him and spoke cheerfully, 'It's all right. I've got a wooden leg below the knee ; all he got was a splinter in his tooth.' At my sister's place on the Potomac, Kiki had a sun stroke ; unhappily it wasn't fatal. When we returned to Washington, Kate departed to New York for a few days before we sailed leaving Kiki in my charge. I gave him to my aunt and only reached New York too late to do anything about it. My aunt gave the creature to a retired Admiral, and Kiki lived to a ripe old age attended by a darky valet.

The first night at Villa d'Este on Lake Como, Kate and I went down to dinner quite late. At a table in the room I saw an old schoolmate, Woods Plankinton, and his wife. Woods looked up, gave a start and cast his eyes down. I tackled him after dinner and he explained that he hadn't heard I was married, so when he saw me come in with a pretty girl he was properly discreet.

We had been in Como perhaps ten days when a cable arrived from the State Department. 'You are assigned Third Secretary to the Embassy at London.' At the same moment a cable arrived for my wife from a close friend and musical enthusiast in Washington, 'Congratulations, so glad, now you can carry on your music.' I was young enough to suspect unwarranted interference with my own affairs and to resent it.

Furthermore, in those days the principal job of the Third Secretary in a big Embassy was to array oneself properly and to distribute the Ambassador's cards about the city ; also to be available in case a guest for dinner fell out at the last minute. So I cabled William Phillips, who had just become Third Assistant Secretary, requesting the assignment be held up until my return to Washington. It was cancelled. I didn't dream we were on the verge of a European war. Had I accepted, the chances are I should have remained in London during the war years and lived through the war on the Allied side. Instead I missed two years of the conflict and then viewed it from the side of Germany. Probably my deep interest in Central Europe would never have grown, and the rest of my life could well have been radically different. Whether for better or worse I do not know. It is fortunate we do not realize in advance the magnitude of often trivial decisions. If we did so we would go through life torn by an agony of doubt. As events have shaped themselves, Kate and I have never regretted the decision, though we might have been tempted to choose otherwise had we had prevision of the next six months.

Back in Chicago we rented a little house on the grounds of the Glen View Club, where I proceeded to turn my wife into a golfer. She was interested in the preliminary stages, the purchase of clothes and golfing equipment, but failed to be bitten by the mania even though she was able to hit quite a stout drive. I was obliged to learn the first great lesson of matrimony, namely, that each partner must accept the other as he or she is, and not try to remake them ; that you have made your choice of a person grown and formed and not of a plastic clay figure. The experiment failed of turning a singer into a golfer.   And I must admit that she was a lot better singer than I was golfer.

We visited my wife's family in Ann Arbor.   Professor Bogle, my father-in-law, was a striking figure, well over six feet in height, with a shock of snow-white wavy hair, a slow-spoken, able conversationalist with a dry humor.   I saw little of him in my life but admired him thoroughly.   He was a practising lawyer as well as Professor in the Law Faculty of Michigan University, and I have frequently met former students who admired him intensely and spoke with deep gratitude of his influence on their study and on their lives.

My sister Mary put at our disposal her house on the Potomac River ; since I had to be in Washington through part of June and July, we took it with gratitude.   It was blazing hot, but the old house was spacious and at least better than the heat radiating from the asphalt streets of the city.   Our black Emma was there and made us extraordinarily comfortable. Emma is almost my first recollection, a short figure dressed in rustling taffeta, round and comfortable.   She was a part of our family considerably before I was, my mother having brought her from Virginia long before I was born.   On my mother's death Mary, as the oldest child, had, so to speak, inherited Emma.   Emma had bullied us, washed our ears, and taken care of us all, and when put to it she was a cook of genius.   She adopted my wife as part of the family, called her 'Mrs. Hugh,' and used to bring her egg-noggs of excellent quality.   My wife asked how they were made.   'Well, Mrs. Hugh,' said Emma, 'I takes a bit of brandy, some milk, a little nutmeg, an aig, and I tops it all off with a "mosquito" cherry.' Emma avoided the usual pitfalls and never allowed any designing male to marry her for her money, so when she died a few years ago she had quite a sum collected, invested on advice of my brother-in-law.   During her lifetime she had already built herself a memorial window in her local church which she enjoyed for some years before she died.   Her will showed that she had divided her property among the children of my brothers and sisters and myself.   I don't think Emma thought of herself as a servant ; certainly we children never thought of her as such.   She was a member of the family with full rights, privileges, and authority.

I was told in the Department somewhat apologetically that I was returning to Latin America, not to Guatemala, but to Buenos Aires.   I didn't mind.   I had enjoyed what I had seen of Latin America and rather anticipated a further experience there.   Also I knew that it was customary to maintain only one Secretary in the Embassy and preferred a place where I would have some responsibility and a chance perhaps to be Chargé d'Affaires for a period.   So I accepted happily enough, and we set about our preparations.

It was during the period at my sister's house on the Potomac in Virginia that I read of the assassination of the Archduke Ferdinand at Sarajevo.   I must confess that the event raised no great apprehension in my mind.   The little thought I gave the matter led me to feel that the Austrians should really be stiff with a group of people who would sympathize with political murder.   Even after my period in Paris I had no real conception of the political commitments of Europe and their ramifications, and was sure that any trouble could be localized. Besides, they had been crying 'Wolf' so often in the Balkans during recent years that I had reached the point of discarding that region as the origin of a great conflict, even if the latter should come. So we went ahead with tranquil minds making our preparations to sail from New York to Southampton, thence to Buenos Aires. Our boat was to sail August 1. Towards the latter part of July the storm seemed about to break, and we consulted as to whether we should carry out our plans. But even in those days it seemed to us the storm would be confined, if it came, to Central Europe. A stretch of the imagination together with a knowledge of the French-Russian alliance, might lead to the fear of France becoming involved. The wildest stretch did not include England.

News of the German ultimatum came the night before we sailed. We dined in the roof-garden at the Ritz that night with a party of friends. At the table next to us and talking with great animation was Count Bernstorff, the German Ambassador. I remember we said to each other how we wished we could overhear what he was saying. I have seen quite a bit of Count Bernstorff since that time and it is my considered opinion that he has been shockingly misjudged by the American public. He struggled hard to present the German case to America, he defended measures of which he often disapproved. He was a German and a diplomat and, as a patriot and a representative of his Government, he could not do otherwise than what he did. He might easily have done it much less well; I doubt if anyone could have done it better. He did his utmost, at decided personal risk, but to no avail, to keep his country from a policy which would bring the United States into the war. In the German Republic he became a leading member of the Demokratische Partei, the party which held ideals closer to ours than did any other German political organization. He saw his party share the fate of many other moderate and middle groups, slowly disintegrate to the right and the left. He was Germany's representative through the long diplomatic struggle of the Preparatory Commission for Disarmament at Geneva, and he fought sturdily for the equality of rights that Germany was finally conceded after his retirement and ultimately realized for itself. He fought three great fights, all of them losing fights, but he always fought gallantly, and he always fought patriotically.

Billy Moorhead, a classmate at Yale, saw me off. We leaned on the rail and wondered whether there was any chance that we might be dragged into the war. Here came a first flash of foresight ; we feared that if the war went on too long interference with our commerce might get us involved. But it was remote conjecture and many months were to pass before we lost any sleep over it. On the trip Kate and I quickly became members of a group which ate at the same table and played bridge together. The others were three young men — one a Britisher returning to join his regiment of lancers, one an Austrian, one a Hungarian, also returning to their military posts. The five of us discussed the war, without hostility but with excitement and perhaps a feeling of awe, particularly when the news came, first of the invasion of Belgium, then of Great Britain's entry. These three young men, about to fight on opposing sides, made little jokes about how long it would be before they could speak to each other again. On August 7th we pulled into Southampton, the last passenger ship to enter that port. Soldiers lined the wharf. We rode up to London and drove through a very quiet city to the Savoy Hotel.

CHAPTER VIII

London was packed. The hotel itself was full of excited Americans, Argentines and others whose plans had been upset by the war. All seemed intent on sailing away at the earliest possible date from this Europe which had suddenly gone mad and betrayed them. I hastened to my own steamship office and asked for news of the departure of the *Alcántara*, on which I had booked passage. I was told that the Admiralty had taken over the entire shipping of the nation for the uses of the Expeditionary Force ; that the *Alcántara* might sail for South America next week, next month, or next year. Nobody knew anything. I realized from the conversations in the Savoy that the Embassy must be extraordinarily driven, so called at Grosvenor Gardens to offer my services until the Admiralty should release a boat and I could sail for Buenos Aires.

I pushed my way through crowded corridors into Ned Bell's office, told him I was ready to help and was greeted with great enthusiasm. Ned said they had dozens of volunteers but none except myself qualified by law to perform official acts, so I could work with another Secretary, Gerry Greene, in the passport office which they were going to establish in the Savoy Hotel. He dragged me in to Mr. Page's office ; the Ambassador was delightful, and I felt to the full that extraordinary charm and confidence which he inspired in all who came into touch with him. He was under no illusion about the struggle which was beginning. He expected a long and bitter war ;

indeed, he was the first person that I had met who gave me even an impression of the magnitude of what was to take place.

The room in the Savoy where Gerry Greene and I set up our office was called 'Patience.' Whoever baptized it had an eye on future necessities. Patience was the quality our visitors needed in abundance. Gerry and I worked as rapidly as we could, but it was slow going. None of this travelling throng had a passport, few had any documents to establish their identity beyond calling cards and letters of credit. Sometimes a check-book on an American bank had to suffice. We relied a good bit on accent and cross examination, though the first was no use in the case of naturalized citizens and the second of little value if the applicant came from, or claimed to come from, cities which we did not know. I often thought subsequently of what a blessing our office must have been to any intelligent spy. His first step in getting evidence of American citizenship must have been so easy with our haphazard issue of papers. For a few days our visitors crowded the room and clamored for attention. Then with the help of some Boy Scouts that trouble was eliminated. Double rows of gilt ballroom chairs were arranged down a long corridor. Scouts issued numbers to applicants in order of arrival, and no one was allowed to enter 'Patience' until his number was called. All they could do was to sit and reflect on the word painted over the doorway. When an applicant was called and left his seat, the crowd rose and moved one chair nearer the door, rather like a solemn game of 'musical chairs.'

On the floor below us was another American office, set up to help travellers. We heard remarkable stories of the organizing ability of one man on the Committee, a mining engineer named Herbert Hoover. Our task was simple compared to theirs. The Americans who flocked in there wanted money, steamboat accommodations, the arrival of the American fleet. They wanted the Committee to recover trunks left in Prague ; to get back a set of furs paid for in Leipzig, but not delivered ; to communicate with friends in various parts of the Continent. Above all they wanted comfort ; they wanted to talk it over and tell their troubles. They wanted to know why their summer playground had risen in fury. They felt a bit as a child does if the good old family St. Bernard should suddenly show his teeth and growl. No experience of my life has so emphasized to me the spiritual remoteness of our people from Europe. The peoples on the Continent were more or less expecting war and even though in England the man on the street may have been stunned by it, he was not profoundly surprised ; too many years full of its threat had made him accustomed to the idea. But to the American, even to the travelled one, the war came as something unbelievable, something for which no training had prepared him, something towards which he felt personally resentful.

In rare intervals of leisure I would look out of the windows of 'Patience' across the Embankment to the Thames. The same Thames flowed by when the British Expeditionary Forces were giving battle at Crécy and Agincourt, at Ramillies and Waterloo, but did the Black Prince or Marlborough or Wellington have the same enormous responsibility as the men directing affairs in England now ? Certainly contemporary literature shows that England during the wars of Louis XIV and Napoleon went about its daily business and that the normal existence of the English subject was little disturbed. But

already England had changed in this war ; Kitchener was appealing for volunteers by the hundreds of thousands, industry
was being diverted to munitions, shipping was being taken
over, the man on the street was filled by the menace to the
very existence of his land.   For what had happened was stupendous.   The Germans had battered down the forts of Liége
and Namur like cardboard, a million men had poured into
Belgium ; the British were undergoing terrific punishment
somewhere south of Mons.   This was no continental adventure to redress the balance of power ; this was a struggle for
existence in which every resource of the nation must be involved.   Those were sombre days through August and the
first days of September.   We read of 20,000 men being killed
in action ; 20,000 men, it was the population of Evanston when
I was a boy there.   Then came the Battle of the Marne, the
first check to German arms.   Enthusiasm was heightened by
the picturesque use of Paris taxis to transport Galliéni's army
towards the Marne.   It lent almost a touch of comedy to the
drama to picture an endless row of rattletrap taxis, coughing
and sputtering, carrying warriors to battle.   After the Marne
the task would be long and arduous, but the German armies
had been beaten once, and all England settled down to it.

In the meantime my wife had been busy at Maple's and elsewhere getting together a household for us.   We were to get
the house on arrival at our post and then send for everything,
so she made her purchases subject to confirmation by cable,
stocking a phantom house and relying only on an active imagination.   We had both led nomadic existences for some years
previously and had few possessions.   As for me, I had ac-
counted it an advantage to own nothing which could not be

put into a trunk and a couple of suit-cases. I was somewhat aghast when I saw the amounts of things that were necessary to furnish a house, but Kate insisted that I would like it infinitely better than taking furnished accommodations, and she was entirely right. My part in furnishing the house consisted in purchasing a quantity of books and stocking the eventual wine cellars.

I have searched my memory for my impressions of those days, but it is difficult to recover them. The whole world has read so much about the period that it is nearly impossible to know what is subsequently acquired knowledge and what was available at the time. To cite one example : of the British Cabinet in 1914, Grey, Asquith, Churchill, and Lloyd George have all written memoirs, and their thoughts have overlaid our original impressions ; hundreds of histories, magazine articles, novels and sketches have treated the first weeks of the war. I can remember my bewilderment, my awe, my fear too, I admit, and my puzzled ignorance of what it was all about. I remember thinking savagely of the limitations of my knowledge, of the vast forces of which I must be ignorant. The various apologias of the different governments were unconvincing. This gigantic thing could not have begun through the blundering of one Kaiser ; there must be more to it than that, but I did not understand enough to know what it was. The tales of atrocities began to reach London ; they increased my angry bewilderment. I couldn't believe one side all white and the other all black ; it was against common sense and against human experience. I am glad I have no diary for the period. I might add here that all my papers were destroyed in the great earthquake and fire in Tokyo in 1923.

If I had a diary and were honest enough to reproduce the pages relating to those days, they would show little penetration, few profound observations ; they would show bewilderment, deep distress, and angry questions. I am glad I haven't one because I might well be tempted to improve it by suppression and addition. I have read many a diary of times of great crises which left me thoroughly skeptical ; in a period of intense bewilderment and questioning, major prophets must be a small proportion of the population. Yet the publication of diaries seems to prove the contrary. Sometimes the diaries are so patently honest that the writer seems puerile. I can think of a puerile diary and a major prophet diary both dealing with the opening days of the Russian revolution and know which of the two authors I consider an honest man. Diaries are useful for detail, excellent for the light they shed on the circumstances surrounding decisions. Nevertheless, their value is nearly always indirect ; in other words, the motives and foresight that a man attributes to himself are seldom as accurate as his reporting of another's stated word. A man's analysis of his own motives, even to the privacy of his diary, is as specious a bit of pleading as an attorney makes to the Court for his client.

Towards the end of September a note from the steamship office announced that the *Alcántara* would sail from Liverpool on the 29th. We nearly missed the boat train. We had mountains of luggage, taxis were rare and our decrepit vehicle moved so slowly that we had only a couple of minutes to spare at the station. Here there was only one porter and a small truck. My wife, the taxi driver and I all seized things and rushed for the platform, just reaching the train. When we caught our breath Kate turned on me with amused exasperation and pointed out that I had saved my golf bag and had been quite ready to abandon her hat-box.

During the first days at sea rumors of enemy raiders were prevalent. German submarines had not yet begun their activities, but some of the surface craft that had not been able to return to a German port were doing what damage they could before their inevitable capture. Our ship ran at night without lights, portholes closed and shuttered. We went to bed one night expecting to awaken in the Tagus River off Lisbon. Early in the morning, well before dawn, a violent crash followed by splintering steel awoke the ship. The vessel rolled slowly over until things spilled about the cabin, then slowly righted itself. We hurriedly put on bath robe and slippers, seized the jewel-case, and dashed up the companionway. The stairs led direct into the grand saloon where the passengers were milling about in all stages of undress. We were already frightened and fear was heightened by the sound of rushing water outside. The doors to the deck were locked, some of the passengers began to beat on them and scream, panic seemed inevitable, passengers were seizing chairs to smash the windows which led to the deck. The great doors opened and the Captain entered. He assured us there was no danger ; we had been rammed by a French cruiser which was now standing by as indicated by winking signal lights. Both ships had been cruising without lights thus unaware of the proximity of each other. Fortunately, the Captain continued, we had struck over the water line and the plates had buckled on two forward cabins. Again, fortunately, these were the only two empty cabins on the boat ; they had been held for passengers embarking at Lisbon. The rush of water we heard came from the hoses the sailors had been using to wash the decks. At the crash they had dropped the hoses and forgotten to turn off the water. The passengers were quickly reassured, but at least I know the initial scenes and fears of a disaster at sea.

Our boat put in at Rio de Janeiro. Words cannot exaggerate the beauty of the harbor. Everyone who sees it tries to tell about it. I shall be the exception and shall keep the scene in my memory for my own satisfaction. My former Chief, Edwin Morgan, met us at the wharf and, as we had a few hours before our boat put to sea again, drove us about the town and took us to his house in Petropolis in the hills. Mr. Morgan had left Lisbon shortly after my departure. In 1912 he became Ambassador to Rio. There he stayed until 1932 when he resigned. In spite of his twenty years of service there, or perhaps because of it, he continued to live in Rio after he ceased to be Ambassador.

A few days later we went on deck in the early morning and looked upon a flat yellow sea. No land in sight but the boat was proceeding swiftly along a lane bordered on both sides by bell buoys. We were in the estuary of the Rio de la Plata and approaching Buenos Aires.

The city was in the depths of depression. The sudden outbreak of war, and the consequent dislocation of shipping had paralysed commerce. Prices of wheat, sugar, and cattle had collapsed. The war had not continued long enough to cause the enormous demand for raw materials which later set in. I had listened somewhat apprehensively to tales of the expense of Buenos Aires, but from this point of view, the situation, at least temporarily, was not so difficult. Living was no higher than in most great cities of the United States. Nor did the housing situation present any especial trouble. I have always wanted to live entirely outside of a big city if possible ; if not possible, then really in the centre of it. There was a residential part of the town called Belgrano, but to me it had all the disadvantages of a city without the virtue of accessibility. So when we were shown a new apartment building on the Plaza San Martín, a few hundred yards from the Chancery, and across the square from the Hotel Plaza, it appeared to fit our needs. We cabled to London to ship the purchases. A wire came announcing the shipment by a certain boat. Three days later the news was published of the destruction of this ship by a German raider. We passed some days of agitation before we learned that a ship of the same line and of a similar name had been sunk and that our cases were duly approaching the harbor. We went out and purchased kitchen chairs and table and a couple of servants' beds and moved into the flat. The furniture fitted beautifully ; we were very happy in it.

Again I was in a post which made no abnormal calls on my time and energy. The war had not yet brought mutual problems to the Argentine and the United States. We were still talking about the classification of tinned salmon in the Argentine tariff and the introduction of Argentine hides into the United States. I began work on Spanish more seriously than I had done in Guatemala, and gradually I developed a real liking for the tongue. Things can be expressed so amusingly in Spanish, at the same time the language is so logical and simple. It is years since I have spoken it, but I have always maintained that it is a pity that the world cannot be persuaded to adopt Spanish as a general second language. Every word is spelled as pronounced ; exceptions to grammatical rules are practically non-existent. All who study it as well as other tongues, are impressed with the relative ease of learning it. It has a great literature, a great drama, a great history, and it represents a great civilization.

I once said something of this kind to Mrs. Dave Morris, one of the leaders in the Esperanto movement. She replied that experience has shown that jealousy between nations would never permit the choice of a language already in existence for the common one. It is a pity. It would be a great advantage to take a living language with tradition and dignity behind it, instead of an artificial one however exact and easy. I left Mrs. Morris convinced that no living language would serve. Nevertheless I regret it. I would like to think that every educated man had, through knowledge of a common language and civilization, a cultural sympathy which educated men in the Middle Ages found in Latin and its literature.

George Lorillard was Chargé d'Affaires, a man of intelligence, an unusual linguist ; he was one of the most anti-social men I have known. He waged war on humanity with a kind of fierce independence. He drew a circle about his life which he permitted no one to cross and an endeavor to cross it met with studied rebuff. He said to me just before the arrival of the new Ambassador, when we had worked together perhaps a month, 'I am not bad when I am on my own. You will have seen that my work is pretty competent, but as soon as the Ambassador arrives I will be no use whatever, and you will have to do everything. I can't work under anybody.' It was all true.

Colonel, now General, Brainard, was the Military Attaché.

Brainard was a man of remarkable record.   He enlisted in the Army as a young man, fought in the plains against the Indians where he lost an eye in a skirmish in the late seventies.   He accompanied Greeley in his trip to the North and was one of three survivors of that unhappy expedition.   As the strongest of the survivors, he staggered out of the camp when he heard the sounds of the rescue party, endeavored to salute at their approach.   Someone thrust a biscuit into his hand, and he never finished the salute.   He was a thick-set, upright figure with a military moustache.   Brainard had a sense of humor and a lovable nature.   I grew fond of him and we made an expedition together which I shall relate later.   I saw Brainard in the street in Washington a couple of years ago. Twenty years had not changed him ; he looked as if he had left the Argentine yesterday.

To our right and to our left on the Plaza San Martín were two immense buildings.   They looked like institutions but were the private homes of the Anchorena and Paz families. The latter house was so big and so imposing that we always spoke of it as the 'Poor House.'   We visited Mme. de Gainza there and approached her salon through a series of five or six large reception rooms, each holding one superlatively beautiful object : a tapestry, a Ming vase, or a picture.   Every room was decorated with restraint, but each showed to advantage some lovely thing of distinction.   When the sun came through the windows and lighted the rugs and tapestries, that series of rooms made a memorable picture.

There were numerous houses in the city of the same spacious dimensions.   When the children of Argentine families married, they did not immediately set up their own households ;

they merely lived under the same roof as their parents, as did their children when they married.   I often went to one house where four generations lived, the great-grandmother who had come to the capital from the land, her daughter, her daughter's children, and their children.   These relatively few families of huge incomes still kept to a singular degree the patriarchal form of family life that they had acquired through generations on the land.   When you visited their ranches, or 'estancias,' you could see from the additions and irregularities of the house how it had been added to through generations to give space for growing families.   Even when they came to the city this habit prevailed.   Hence, when we were invited to dinner we seldom sat down less than thirty even for an informal family meal.

The house of our doctor was a picture gallery in itself.   He had a beautiful collection of which he was rightly proud, and he loved showing it and discussing the pictures.   Rumor had it that each picture represented the fee that he had obtained for some successful case.   Kate was being treated by him the first time he showed us his collection, and I remember reflecting apprehensively as to whether he was going to assess me for a Van Dyck or would let me off for a Cézanne or a Corot.   The wife of another doctor in the city had a magnificent house.   She had approximately ten children, looked about twenty-five years old and was pretty as a picture.   When she received you in spacious and perfectly appointed reception rooms, in an atmosphere of calm and luxury, it seemed incredible that an army of children existed under the roof.   We always reassured ourselves by asking to see them.   A whole row of the little things were led in by the governess, all starched, ruffled and curled.

When we arrived, late in October, the weather was just getting warmer. It grew hotter and hotter until by Christmas it was something that I had never before felt. Since then I have lived summers in Washington and Tokyo so that I know there are other summers equally bad. Then I was sure that the Argentine summer was the worst. We baked while the grass grew brown and the leaves withered. Then we read in the papers that, miles in the interior, a swarm of locusts had arrived and were moving in our direction. They gradually approached the city, the newspapers published reports of their coming, rather like cyclone bulletins in Florida. Eventually they enveloped the town. They were everywhere in incredible numbers. They ate the grass, they ate the leaves, they ate the flowers. When they flew it was like a cloud passing. People beat tin pans in their gardens to scare them into other people's gardens. Gangs of men dug ditches in the country before their advance and buried millions. Still they came. They covered the sidewalks as you walked and stared at you with pop-eyes. Your shoes went 'crunch' as you walked on them. The smell of them was everywhere. You smelt them in your clothes, in your hair, in the food you ate. They moved on like every other trouble in life.

The city is a splendid example of modern city construction, the streets spacious, the façades harmonious. The parks and gardens are kept in impeccable order. The race-track is the last word in race-tracks, the Jockey Club the last word in downtown clubs. But with all that the city has one provincialism which I found endearing. Everywhere that I have seen Spanish civilization, from Madrid to the small town in Guatemala, there has been somewhere in the town, usually in

the park around the bandstand, an afternoon 'paseo' or promenade of the young men. Buenos Aires was no exception. In
the late afternoon the Calle Florida, the smartest shopping
street, was roped off against vehicles of all kinds while the
youth of the town made their paseo and the instincts of Spanish civilization were satisfied. The prevailing costume was
black. Even when families were not in mourning, men and
women were likely to clothe themselves in black. The result was excessively smart if somewhat sombre. The city is
built on a flat plain ; there is no natural beauty in the vicinity.
When you leave the city you enter the plain. I never had a
motor in Buenos Aires ; there was no place to go except elsewhere in the city. If you wanted to leave for the week-end,
you either took an all-night train to Mar del Plata, a sort of
Newport, or an all-night steamer to Montevideo. Travel both
ways was very comfortable, however, and beautiful beaches
and surf bathing were at the end of either trip.

Spanish formalism was rigidly respected in the time of
which I write, although I understand that social customs and
taboos have been much relaxed in the past twenty years. At a
ball I might dance with the young ladies, but no young man
might dance with my wife. She was obliged to sit in a solemn
row with the other married women and enjoy the gaiety vicariously. After some months of silent revolt my wife danced
with one of the Secretaries of the French Embassy. He duly
led her back to her seat, bowed, thanked her and retired. An
older Argentine woman of our acquaintance came over to Kate
and said, 'My dear, you have such a good reputation, do not
spoil it by doing what is against our custom.' If my wife were
alone on the street and a young man of her acquaintance

passed, he did not speak to her, apparently he would only salute if she were accompanied. Curiously, many of the Argentine families spent months of each year in Paris and London where they lived the normal social life of the city. As soon as they returned to Buenos Aires, however, they were scrupulous in observing the old forms. One or two of the younger Argentine married women tried to lead the life they led in Europe, but they were so bitterly criticized that it seemed hardly worth while.

The opera season was excellent. The Argentines had the same insistence for the best-known stars as the American public. Productions were lavish ; so was the audience. I have never seen elsewhere such a blaze of diamonds. Caruso, Scotti, Geraldine Farrar, and Galli-Curci were all there, and Rosa Raisa made her debut. We went constantly. If we didn't have tickets ourselves we were asked by the Argentines who loved to entertain in this pleasing way. Tickets for the President's box were often sent to the Embassy, and we had to arrange a party hastily to fill it.

Just now I became acquainted for the first time with the idiosyncrasy of government in repect to monetary matters. An instruction came from Washington that my salary was docked for three weeks because I had taken more than the statutory period to proceed to Buenos Aires from Washington. Useless to protest that the British Admiralty, which had taken all ships for the expeditionary forces, was to blame and not I. Futile to add that Mr. Page, our Ambassador, had been good enough to write thanking me for being of real help during those rush days at London. The Department was adamant, the regulations so read, and so they must be applied.

Every man in the service has been through his troubles in this respect ; no group of them get together without exchanging anecdotes as to endless argument with the Bureau of Accounts over some interpretation of travel regulations. The same is true of the Army and Navy, and of every other Government official. Vast numbers of persons are in the employ of the Government, and for each one there must be prepared and turned in a bewildering number of printed forms of expenditure. Another army, I don't know the size, must pore over these papers, analyse and study them. New forms constantly arrive and further bewilderment ensues. In spite of the forms, the clerical effort, the army of checkers, I am convinced that an ingenious crook in Government employ would find that beating the Government was as easy as stealing cash from a blind man's cup.

CHAPTER IX

The new Ambassador, the first Ambassador of the United States to the Argentine, Mr. Frederic Stimson, of Dedham, near Boston, arrived with his wife shortly after we did. Mr. Stimson was a Professor of Constitutional Law, an author of novels and political commentary, a man of great charm and distinction. He talked interestingly, his humor was unfailing and sometimes puckish. He was tall, thin, his hair grey and beard pointed. He came to be known in Buenos Aires, where nearly everybody earns a nickname, as 'Jesus in a dress-suit.' His wife came from Philadelphia. She was intelligent and also of great distinction. She read enormously and discussed what she read with passionate interest. They took a comparatively small house in the section of Belgrano ; in that city of vast expenditure they had neither the means to live lavishly nor the inclination had they had the means. They lived simply and contributed from the spirit and not from the pocket. It did not take the Argentines long to appreciate their rarity. They sensed their distinction. In any gathering these two people were personages. The French have a phrase I would have used for Mr. Stimson. 'Il était un Monsieur,' which, I assure you, is a great deal more than being called a 'gentleman.'

Mr. Stimson had a habit, however, under which many a hostess has suffered. At the dinner table he would help himself generously (another point in his favor — he loved good food) and then begin to discourse most engagingly or inter-estingly or both. The other guests would listen, but they would also finish their dishes. Mr. Stimson would end his re-marks in leisurely fashion, pick up his fork and begin his food with equal leisure. The guests waited patiently, the hostess waited in anxiety, the cook waited in fury, and the soufflé didn't wait at all — it collapsed. Mr. and Mrs. Stimson both had too much character, were too individual not to clash on occasion ; those clashes were sometimes stimulating to the outsider, and they were always diverting. They were keen bridge players, both spirited bidders, both as individual in the game as they were in their lives. The discussion which fol-lowed the rubber was a battle of wit. There was never a victor or a vanquished.

They were staunch friends to us. Mrs. Stimson was a tower of strength through a serious illness of my wife. Mr. Stimson is our child's godfather. We always visit them in Dedham when we go to Boston.

I had been really apprehensive before the arrival of the Am-bassador, lest in Buenos Aires, a city where great wealth was almost a commonplace, an Ambassador of moderate income should find himself in embarrassment and difficulty. This ap-prehension quickly fled as I saw the immediate recognition by the Argentines of the personalities of Mr. and Mrs. Stimson. Great fortunes are a comfort to an Ambassador. They ease his contact with the people of the country where he is living, and if he can afford constant and generous entertainment, he has a wide opportunity to bring to his house men and women of interest and value to his work. As I think of my Chief in the Argentine, however, and of others whom I met later, I recognize that great wealth merely eases the path, it does not insure success. Relations with people who really count, in contrast to the merely social group, come from the ability to interest them, to talk to them intelligently about their own affairs and has little or no relation to the scale on which the Ambassador is living. He can seldom live on his salary alone in a way that is dignified, nor can he on his salary pay the many unavoidable obligations that accrue to his position. In most posts, if he is dependent on his salary, he must be constantly embarrassed by the thought that he is receiving more than he is giving. But also in most posts, the difference between his salary and the amount sufficient to enable him to feel at ease, is not overwhelming. Few of us in the Service believe that salaries of Ambassadors should be increased. We would much prefer to see allotments for entertaining, for which accounts should be rendered. A modest beginning has been made in this direction, but as yet the allotments are so insufficient in the posts where demands are heavy that the choice of men to fill them must fall on those who can make up the deficiency from their personal income. Our great Democracy must rely on an undemocratic criterion when choosing its representatives.

Americans are invariably surprised when they begin to inquire into this matter. They find that our Ambassadors and Ministers are obliged to carry really heavy expenses from their own purses for entertainments that the traveller had assumed were borne by the Government. I know of many instances where American travellers have telephoned their representatives on days of national festivals to ask what provision is made by the Ambassador for their entertainment. They are always horrified subsequently to learn that the Ambassador is paying for the entertainment himself and that they have thrust themselves on his hospitality. Official entertainment of Government officers and diplomats of other countries cannot be avoided ; it is as indispensable to their tasks as is the entertainment that a salesman gives his customer, and no employer in business would fail to recognize the necessity and make allowance for it. Americans are startled also to find that all the other great countries of the world and even most of the smaller ones take cognizance of the need for adequate entertainment allowances and make due provision for their representatives. Foreigners, on the other hand, are surprised when they learn of the treatment which the great American Republic accords its officers in this respect. Such thoughts as these began to come to me as I watched the career of my Chief in Buenos Aires.

Manuel Erraúsquin came to see me soon after our arrival, and we saw much of him and liked him. He and I had both been keen about the same girl in Chicago ; our affection for the lady had been at different times so a feeling of rivalry had never developed, rather our common memory and appreciation of each other's good taste was a bond of sympathy. We often went to the races with Erraúsquin as my wife is an enthusiastic if not very successful gambler. Whenever she appeared to be in particularly bad luck, which was nearly every time, Erraúsquin would climb to a box full of grey-headed Jockey Club members. There he would take counsel with his father, an owner of stables and inveterate follower of the sport. He would return, report the result of his investigations and sometimes the day was saved.

The racing was very good, excellent horses and jockeys and a course in the pink of condition.   One of the best restaurants in the city was in the Jockey Club reservation.   As I remember the arrangement, the Municipality leased the racing privilege to the Club ; by the terms of the concession the Club was under obligation to hold races twice a week through the entire year.   I have seen races where the horses wallowed through three inches of water standing on the track, also where they raised a cloud of dust that was not as dense as the cloud of locusts that swarmed over them.   To tell the truth, I became a little tired of the races.   Once I saw a scene in a play ; a man was being urged by his wife to go to the movies and see Tom Mix in a Wild West picture.   He refused, she insisted. At last, goaded into a fury, he sprang to his feet and shouted, 'I won't go to the movie.   I never want to see Tom Mix again in all my life.   I must have seen that guy ride a hundred thousand miles.'   Poor fellow ; I thought of the Buenos Aires races, and my heart bled for him.

In posts where the civilization of the country is alien to western standards, diplomats see a great deal of other members of the diplomatic corps.   In Peking, for example, the Corps is like a great club ; diplomats who have been to Peking and meet each other elsewhere feel an immediate sympathy and interest.   In most small posts as well, the diplomatic body becomes well acquainted.   But in large cities of western civilization or in one of western origin, the contrary is the case ; the Corps is widely scattered, meets officially only once or twice a year and mingles more with the society of the city itself and less with its colleagues.   This was certainly the case in Buenos Aires.   The thin, bearded face of Sir Reginald Tower, the

British Ambassador, was sometimes at our table, and I remember at his house being introduced to his parrot of remarkable vocabulary. Graf Luxburg, the German Representative, later sprang into world notoriety as the author of the telegram which was intercepted and deciphered with its damning phrase of 'spurlos versenkt.' He was a sardonic talker with a wit which devastated his adversaries, a real intelligence. Apart from the moral question, I have never understood how his intellect permitted him to go on record as advocating 'sinking without a trace,' even in a supposedly confidential message to his Government. Proskowitz, the Austro-Hungarian Chargé d'Affaires, however, we saw often. He was a bachelor and lived in one room of the vast Embassy, big enough to house a regiment. When I went to see him I marched through endless rooms, furniture and pictures covered with sheets, my footsteps re-echoing loudly.

Kate, Proskowitz, Lorillard and I went to Montevideo for a week-end as a syndicate. We had figured that on the roulette table in the Casino it was possible to make a killing with little capital by means of a system so simple we wondered why no one else had tried it. I was to play the system while the others watched. I wish I hadn't forgotten the system. I would like to divulge it for the protection of others. I played twenty-five turns, our maximum. Our capital had disappeared without one favorable turn. But we had a joyful trip to Montevideo.

Proskowitz had property in eastern Austria-Hungary — in Galicia, I think. As the news of the fighting on the eastern front came to Buenos Aires, I used to visit him. He had large-scale maps, knew the area and could expound the names and topography of this, to me, unknown region. The war, of course, divided the diplomats into separate camps which could not meet. That may be a further reason why I saw them so little and remember them so vaguely.

I wish I could avoid discussing the war, but even in the far-off Argentine, its shadow was cast over us, and though we were leading normal lives, our thoughts were never free from the tremendous tragedy. I did not want Great Britain and France to be beaten. I knew France a bit — better than most Americans — I knew something of England and liked what I knew. I knew little of Germany, had an affectionate recollection of South Germany and its people, but of the country as a whole I was ignorant. I didn't want to see France humiliated again at Versailles. But our President had urged us to remain neutral, and I did what I could to understand both sides. As to the origins of the war I was slowly being enlightened. Proskowitz, the Austro-Hungarian, and the Russian Chargé d'Affaires had both served in the Balkans. Repeated conversations with them separately threw a flood of light upon the struggle that had been waged for years between Austria-Hungary and Russia, with occasional intervention by Italy, in that region. The struggle had been silent but tense, had been waged with a lack of scruple and by means which would make the modern thriller read like a Sunday-School tract. I could no more assess a moral responsibility in this murky field than I could between two tom-cats giving battle on a roof. Germany's submarine warfare was causing intense hatred, but would any nation with the means fail to use the weapon, especially when they were being blockaded and their civilian population beginning to feel the pinch of hunger ? Italy's cynical entrance into the war did nothing to clarify the matter of responsibility. The condemnation of Miss Cavell caused a storm, but the storm was raised not by the shooting of a spy — every nation in battle knew the rules of war — but by the character and the purity of patriotic motive of Miss Cavell.

The invasion of Belgium and the violation of neutrality seemed the one unanswerable indictment of Germany. Bethmann-Hollweg had admitted it. 'The wrong we have done Belgium' was the cry of an honest man and from the point of view of consequences, probably the most disastrous admission that a German could have made. But I always came back to the simple conception that I did not want Great Britain and France to lose. This was not reason, this was instinct. If one can argue from the particular to the general, I wonder if this racial and hereditary instinct was not after all the final reason why the United States took the step it did. Have we here another instance of the normal human endeavor to rationalize its conduct and prove to itself that its acts are dictated by mind and not by instincts? Did the whole country want England and France to win and did we look for motives to justify us in helping them? Any one reason for our entry into the war is of course too simple, but if we are to simplify the problem, I submit that my suggestion is more valid and believable than the explanation that one hundred and twenty million Americans went to war to save the investments of a few banking houses.

At that time I was not violent-minded. In the midst of my friends I was not orthodox, though I became so outwardly when we went to war. But my mind never ceased to question, nor did I ever learn to accept *ex parte* statements by one side as the final verity.   To my mind the most revolting thing about war is not the suffering and misery, not the sacrifice of treasure and life ; it is the propaganda that war brings, it is the prostitution of truth to policy, the debasing of truth from an abstract absolutism to a commodity to be rationed to a people in diluted doses calculated to make them docile in following a policy.   We deplore the lack of honesty in present-day government and business, yet what a precedent of dishonesty we all set a score of years ago in propaganda.   We have sown the seeds ; we are reaping the harvest.

I am inclined to think that it is one of the penalties of my profession, the inability to share wholeheartedly in the enthusiasm and hatreds of your own people.   I call it a penalty because it is often a somewhat lonely position to stand, as it were, on the edge of a great national enthusiasm and ever to be beset by argument as to the exactness of its causes.   We have lived in too many lands to enjoy the luxury of international loves and hates, we have studied the causes of too many national movements to condemn them from one side and especially from the outside.   We have learned that each nation of men has a small proportion of men of integrity, an overwhelming proportion of those ordinarily honest but subject to temptation, and a small proportion of rascals.   We find ourselves unable to declare 'This nation is honest,' or 'That nation is a band of crooks.'   We cannot put labels on peoples and states and argue from the premise of those labels.   In international life we are somewhat like the attorney in civil life.   The attorney must examine both sides of a case in which he is interested. He knows the danger of assumption.   He knows that the whole truth seldom rests on one side.   So do we.

We Americans love our enthusiasms and cherish our hatreds. Not only that, but when we come abroad or when we live in a foreign land for the first time, we readily adopt the enthusiasms and hatreds of the foreign land and add them to our own ; we proceed to judge and condemn from the premises of the foreigner as well as from those of our native land. It is the task of a diplomat to avoid such luxuries, to keep his own mind and that of his government, so far as in him lies, on a basis of fact and not assumption, on a path that leads to one goal only, the ultimate good of his nation. Talleyrand's words to the young diplomat were good, 'Surtout, pas trop de zèle.' I shall be bold enough to say that I wish he had added a line of conduct for the youngster to memorize — 'We do not love, we do not hate, we do not judge, we do not condemn ; we observe, we reflect, we report.'

But this is a long way from Buenos Aires. Kermit Roosevelt had married Belle Willard, the daughter of our Ambassador to Spain, and brought her to Buenos Aires where Kermit was working in a bank. They became our very good friends. Belle was very fair, charming and slender. Her apparent frailty belied her character ; she was decisive, intelligent and intellectually vigorous. She used to drive around Buenos Aires the ramshackle Ford that Kermit had bought and that in days before it was usual for women to drive cars in a city. When someone said to her that it was startling to see a delicate girl with that courage, Belle laughed and replied, 'You have to be hard and you have to be strong if you marry a Roosevelt. If you aren't you would be crushed.'

Kermit had the boundless energy of his father. He had the same inexhaustible curiosity about human beings. Once I came across him early one morning in London.   He asked Kate and me to come to the Ritz for tea with him and his wife ; there wouldn't be anyone else there, and we could talk things over. We arrived to find six or eight people.   Within the next half hour some thirty had assembled.   Waiters had rushed around placing chairs and tables and still no Kermit.   He finally arrived breathless and introduced his guests, explaining that we were all people that he had encountered during the day in London.   There was a writer, a member of the Katchentunga expedition, a chap who was contemplating the ascension of Mt. Everest, big game hunters, a taxidermist and representatives of the shipping industry.

One New Year's day my wife was ill in bed, and Kermit and Belle came to call.   I was still in the office.   Kate had a Spanish maid named Valentina.   She had two thumbs to one hand and looked as if she ought to ride a broomstick on windy nights, but she had a fatal lure for the men.   The butler, a Spaniard, was one of her victims.   The cook was another. After the dreadful series of cooks that is the ordinary lot of a newly married couple, we had hired an East Indian.   He was a jewel.   I remember his curries with gratitude to this day. He was spotless, always clad in a white chef's cap and apron. We never discovered what threw oil on the jealous flames of the two men, but suddenly the butler rushed into my wife's bedroom, his head streaming with blood, and cried out that the cook had assaulted him with a knife just as he was arranging the tea table.   Kermit rushed into the bedroom, dragged linen from the closet, tied it round the butler's head, demanded my gun and proceeded to the kitchen, the two girls following and peering anxiously around the corner.   The cook offered no resistance and Kermit marched him down to a policeman. Four days later Kate and I returned to the house one afternoon, let ourselves in with our key, heard sounds of dishes in the kitchen and went out to see who was there as we had been without a cook since the assault. There was the East Indian in white cap and apron, calmly preparing dinner. 'What are you doing here?' demanded my wife.

'They don't prosecute. They let me go, so I come back, I like you.'

'But you are dismissed. You nearly killed the butler.'

Still in his quiet voice he said, 'But I don't hate him any more, so I come back.' We finally persuaded him that we weren't housing a would-be assassin. He sighed, took off his cap and apron, and departed. I hated to see him go.

One of the Argentine houses that we frequented was that of Mme. de Castex. In spaciousness and in the number of people living there, it was typical of Buenos Aires. Mme. de Castex and her married daughter were both called Suzana. The mother, Mme. de Torres, a slight, stiff little figure, ruled them with a rod of iron. Mme. de Torres' greatest joy was going to the kitchen to concoct delicious sweets and watching her guests consume them. She is still alive, I hear, and still vigorous. There was a son, Dr. de Castex, and there were numerous children of the daughter Suzana. There was ample reception room for all generations, and diversion for all ages. Mme. de Castex had an interest in the cinema theatre, had set up a cinema room in her own house and used to show the films to her friends before they were taken to the theatre. It was in the days of continued films where the heroine was left at the end of each section hanging from the cliff by her fingers while the villain

approached knife in hand.   At the beginning of the next week
she was still hanging there.   One film was called the 'Black
Box.'   It lasted for months and always left you breathless.
There was bridge in the card rooms for those who liked it.
This was the special province of Mme. de Torres who liked to
play for a tiny stake and was out to win.   Since my visit to the
Argentine I have always felt that when all other sources of income fail, I shall have one resource in life.   I shall take another
American to the Argentine and play bridge in set games with
the understanding that we never try to win the rubber but
always double our opponents' bids.   I have never seen such
persistent bidders.   They would play the hand at any price.

Mme. de Castex had a deep interest in music.   She was passionately fond of it and used to have members of the opera
company sing in the intimacy of her house.   I have heard
Scotti and Rosa Raisa sing in this informal way and sing on
request of the audience.   Mme. de Alvear, while no longer
singing in public, sang often in these evenings, a relatively
small voice but perfectly placed and trained.   She sang with
singular charm.   My wife was doing a lot of music in those
days.   She had an accompanist three times a week in the afternoon.   Musically minded people used to drop in for tea.
Kate sang sometimes in the house of Mme. de Castex.   On one
occasion we had been invited to dinner, and Kate was to sing
later.   Unfortunately, that very day Kate, who was expecting
her first child some months later, had visited her doctor.   He
had issued an order that on no account was she to do any
further singing under conditions which stimulated her nerv-
ously.   In those days the simple fact of birth was not discussed
as frankly as at present, and my wife, though shy about it,

nevertheless had to take Mme. de Castex into her confidence and called during the afternoon to do so, imploring her at the same time not to give her secret away.   Mme. de Castex was charming, congratulated her, gave her a little present, told her nobody would ask her to sing that night and, above all, promised to keep her secret as silent as the tomb.   We duly arrived for dinner.   I don't know how many were there.   I remember a long vista of faces with Mme. de Castex at one end of the table and Mme. de Torres opposite.   Dessert was passed, champagne was served, Mme. de Castex tapped her glass and rose to her feet while the guests watched in surprised silence. 'My friends,' she said, 'I want you to drink a toast with me. I had intended for you to have the pleasure tonight of listening to Katherine Wilson's lovely voice, but this, alas, is impossible.   I am asking you to drink a toast to Katherine, and only she, her husband and I know what it is all about.'   The guests began to cheer ; strangely enough, they knew what it was all about.   It was not the habit of Argentine men to send flowers to young married women, but flowers came for us in my office all day long the following day, and many from men who had not been present at dinner the night before.   We were congratulated right and left the next time we went out as if we had announced our engagement.   It put an end to Kate's shyness, at least on this topic.

Every boat from the United States brought a group of compatriots, travellers who were accustomed to go to Europe and now had to seek other lands, young men seeking their fortunes, bankers and business men.   Two young chaps just out of Yale turned up with letters of introduction to me.   They had a few hundred dollars, boundless enthusiasm, complete ignorance of Spanish and of business as well. They were charming boys, and we enjoyed seeing them. One day they came to my house quite crestfallen and about to sail back for the United States. They told this experience : after some weeks of investigation they had closed a deal for a cigar factory. They had been shown over the factory by the owner and had noticed that large stocks of tobacco and other materials were in the store room, enough, they thought, to keep them going until they could replenish their depleted capital by some cash sales of their produce. They closed the deal on a Saturday morning, paid their money, and the title to factory and stock changed hands with the understanding that the boys took physical possession on Monday morning. Bright and early they turned up on Monday ready to start business ; the factory was there but the stock had vanished — the former owner had carted it away over Sunday. So the boys were broke and sailing home. I asked them what they had done to recover and they replied that they had taken care of that. One of the boys had had a letter of introduction to Señor Ricardo Aldao, one of the foremost lawyers in Buenos Aires, so they had called on him and asked him to take the case. It was somewhat as if Mr. Charles Evans Hughes when practising in New York had been asked by a complete stranger to accept a case involving a total outlay of some $400. I asked the boys how Señor Aldao had behaved. They replied that he had listened with a lot of sympathy, had laughed and said he would take the case with pleasure.

Among the bankers who came down was a boyhood friend of mine, Hayden Harris of the Harris Trust Company of Chicago. As a little boy and at school Hayden had always been somewhat different from other boys. He kept a tame bear in his back yard, I remember, and we used to feed it strange dishes, experimenting in the interest of science. As a man, Hayden had succeeded in maintaining his individuality. He was lean and awkward, he spoke with a New England drawl. He had a rich, earthy humor, something Lincolnesque about his tales. He took nothing on trust but was completely ready to 'mull,' as he called it, over any hypothesis, no matter how fantastic. During the Peace Conference at Paris in 1919 I encountered Hayden again. He was in the uniform of a corporal, if I remember accurately. He told me he didn't think much of the war, but when the United States went in he 'figured that if you were in a war the thing to do was to think out how you could kill the most folks,' so he enlisted in heavy artillery. He was sent to Italy and spent a year with his unit on the Italian front. At that moment the financial section of the American Delegation were about to send him to Italy on a mission to the Italian Minister of Finance and were engaged in obtaining his demobilization as they felt dubious about his reception by the Italian Minister if he presented himself with a corporal's stripes on his arm.

Hayden had come to Buenos Aires to look over the possibility of the flotation of certain Argentine loans in the American market. His room in the hotel was strewn with reports, financial statements, and volumes of government statistics. Books were piled on the table and bed and stacked in heaps on the floor. But Hayden's methods did not confine themselves to the printed page ; he emphasized the value of visible and living evidence. He had under consideration the matter of a loan secured by the public works of the city of Rosario, higher up on the River Plate, and asked me to go with him while he looked it over. On the way up he expounded his method. According to Hayden, he would look over the public works but this wouldn't tell him much as he was not an engineer. What he really wanted to ascertain was the state of mind of the inhabitants, whether or not they were enjoying prosperity. Hayden said there were several criteria of prosperity, and if all the tests pointed the same way, it was safe to assume prosperity. An engineer could then look over the public works and learn their condition. The criteria were, I think, three in number : (1) you visited the prisons ; if the inmates were treated reasonably well and had a fairly comfortable existence, it indicated surplus money, since in time of stringency the prisoner was the first person to be deprived of adequate comfort ; (2) you visited cemeteries and made a comparison of the type of tombstones and memorials set up this year in comparison with the past ; this was a rough measure of the money in the pocket of the population ; (3) and this the best index : you visited the gay cafés, talked to the girls and learned from them whether the lads had a lot of money to toss around, how the spenders of this year compared with the past. We examined all these criteria and more. I certainly knew the city of Rosario before I left it.

Kermit Roosevelt had purchased two penguins for the New York zoo, and had prevailed on Hayden to take them back on the steamer with him. I went down to the boat to take leave of Hayden, was talking to him on the deck, when we saw Kermit and Belle driving the Ford along the wharf with two peculiar objects in the rumble.   As they passed below us, we made out the two penguins, seated each on his own cake of ice, thus reproducing through the streets of Buenos Aires, and in the rumble of a Ford, those Arctic conditions to which the penguin is accustomed.

CHAPTER X

Colonel Brainard and I became much interested in the account which an American engineer brought to us one day of a trip which he had made across the Continent through the Southern Andes. We determined to make it. We took the train as far as it went. It landed us in the prairies of the State of Rio Negro, in Northern Patagonia. There we hired a motor which showed extraordinary qualities. It took us across the rolling plain on the most rudimentary roads, sometimes a track only, and brought us, after two days of bumping, to the village of Bariloche. Bariloche was a primitive one-street village, like some of our towns in the West, frame houses built on wooden piles to hold them above the ground. It lies on the edge of Lake Nahuelhuapi. The lake reminded me of Lake Lucerne in Switzerland ; it has the same narrow spidery arms reaching into high clefts of the mountains, the same intensely blue water, the same wooded banks. No snow mountains are visible there, however, as the Andes that far South have lost the ruggedness of the range further North and much of its altitude. The shores were untouched and supremely beautiful. Some day I suppose Nahuelhuapi will be the mountain resort for the people of Buenos Aires, the blue water will be dotted with white sails of racing regattas, villas will cover the banks, and little steamboats will ply from bay to bay.

Some years before we got there the Government of the United States had made a gift to the Argentine of a quantity of eggs of rainbow and speckled trout, which were planted in Nahuelhuapi. The fish thrive in those waters. They grow to a size I have never seen elsewhere and were in great abundance both in the lake and in the tributary streams. The place was so little visited that it was rarely, if ever, fished. We had no tackle but managed to buy some hooks and lines and pulled out the trout with worms à la President Coolidge. There was some shooting, a few duck and plover, and innumerable 'martinetta' on the plains, a long-legged bird a bit like a partridge and good eating. Brainard had a method of shooting I have never seen anyone else employ. I said before that he had lost an eye in the Indian wars. The other eye had been damaged. He wore a pair of binoculars slung over his shoulder, watched the birds' flight through the glasses held in his left hand. When the birds were in range, he dropped the glasses, raised his gun and fired. It was unique as a method but really effective. He shot with great accuracy.

In the street of Bariloche I encountered a burly bearded figure dressed in corduroy trousers and high boots. Seeing a stranger, he stopped and presented himself. Dr. Veerhagen is the way I remember the name. He explained that he was Belgian, had a German wife and was a doctor of medicine. He did the little doctoring that was needed in Bariloche. He pointed out his cottage, a log cabin high up the slope above the village, and invited Brainard and me to dine with them that night. We climbed the rocky forest path to his remote dwelling and were charmingly received by them both. The cabin was delightfully furnished, mostly by their own effort, but what was really astonishing was the sight in such a place of a Steinway grand piano. I walked over to it and examined the litter of music which covered it. Brahms predominated, though Wagner was a close second, a somewhat surprising combination of taste. I picked out a piano adaptation of the wood music from Siegfried and remember asking the Doctor to play us that, as it seemed appropriate to a forest cabin. He complied. He played with a mastery of technique and feeling. From Siegfried he went on to more Wagner and eventually to Brahms who I saw was his real passion. His wife called us repeatedly to dinner ; he didn't hear but played on. He had left his cabin, his woods, his remote existence and was back in a civilized world of music where he was spiritually at home.

After dinner we talked. The man's education, and the woman's as well, was comprehensive and sophisticated. There was nothing in which they were not interested. There was no subject on which they could not flame with enthusiasm of argument, with two representatives of the world they had left behind. The doctor said he would never leave that place ; his wife's eyes filled with tears, but she assented. I had learned in Guatemala the unwritten law of remote regions — you must never ask personal questions about a man's past. You may have vivid interests in common, you may range the whole field of abstractions, you may even become friends, but you must never question any man about himself. You must be content with what he volunteers. So, although I was eaten with curiosity, I obeyed the unwritten law and came away unsatisfied. I have often thought of those two lonely, artistic, civilized figures, their intense interest in the world slaked only by rare conversations with strangers, and have wondered how they fared. What brought them with their talents to such an existence, what broke up the life they must have lived and drove

them into exile ?   I can't answer that, but I know that as they
lived in that lovely remote setting, so will they live wherever
they are, and that if they are alive, they still live beautifully.

We crossed the Andes by a variety of conveyances and over
a series of lakes and trails.   We travelled by sailboat and by
rowboat, by donkey and by wagon.   Everywhere it was pleasing, everywhere it was gentle and lovely — until the Chilean
side where we ran under the flank of the stupendous 'Trona-
dor,' a snow mountain of the first magnitude.   We caught a
train for Santiago and travelled through green rolling agricultural land, an agreeable contrast to the dusty plain of South
Argentine.

In Santiago they cherished the name of Henry Fletcher who
had been our Ambassador there.   During our few days' stay
and in the hospitality which that cheerful city offered, the
opening remark of any citizen was something in praise of
Henry.   We went about under the auspices of George Sum-
merlin, our Chargé d'Affaires.   This in itself would have been
sufficient to ensure us a welcome, but the fact that we knew
Henry as well came near to gilding the lily.   John Keena
was Consul General in Valparaiso.   I had known and liked him
in Buenos Aires as well as his curly-headed wife, Eleanor ; it
was a joy to see them again.   We returned by train to Buenos
Aires.

It was late in 1915 or early in 1916 that the Argentine Government held a Pan-American Financial Conference.   The
Embassy was not directly interested in the affair, and I remember it only because of the people in the American Delegation, and because of a party the Ambassador gave at the Jockey
Club.   The party was a huge stag affair which included all the

male members of our Delegation, Argentines, and Delegates of other countries. After spending most of a day arranging the seating, a couple of exalted gentlemen fell out, and the thing had to be done all over while the guests waited. The guests included Senators, Ministers of Finance, Ministers for Foreign Affairs, Chief Delegates, and all to be put in some kind of order. At that time I had not had my subsequent experience with gatherings at Geneva under the League of Nations, and the problem seemed formidable. I called the Argentine Chief of Protocol to help. It was a hot night and our collars and shirts were wilted when the guests eventually came in.

Senator McAdoo, at that time Secretary of the Treasury, headed the American Delegation. He had just married the daughter of President Wilson, and his wife accompanied him to Buenos Aires. She was a charming woman. Andrew Peters and his wife were in the party as was Mr. Paul Warburg. Mr. Warburg was a remarkable man. I was too unskilled in the matters they were discussing to judge of his financial ability, but I could note the deference that his colleagues accorded him and found that in the most complicated discussion it was his explanation in simple phrases which carried conviction. A man of comprehensive culture, he had a share of that melancholy which seems to be the heritage of his race. He spoke not with cleverness but, far better, with wisdom. None of the American Delegates spoke Spanish, but it was thought that the opening address of our Delegation should be delivered in that language. Accordingly, Mr. Warburg wrote out a speech on the boat coming down, had a translator put it into Spanish, proceeded to memorize it and rehearse its pronunciation with the interpreter. I heard him deliver the address in the inaugu-

ral plenary session. He spoke not only readily, but with elo-
quence. It was an exhibition of dramatic art. When the
session was over I found Mr. Warburg getting into a taxi. I
had to tell the driver to go to the hotel ; Mr. Warburg's
Spanish did not go that far. He was a citizen of the world.
Nothing human was foreign to him, and his doctrine was
moderation. He used to talk to me of his conception of life,
and the word 'moderation' was often on his lips.

I have had to wait a long time to hear again of moderation
as a conscious philosophy, but recently Hilton in his *Lost
Horizon* made moderation the conception of Shangri-la. A
cinema version of that book has just been produced. I rather
regret it. The beauty of line and thought is as fragile and
brittle as the notes of a carillon on a still and frosty night, and
as easily shattered. Can a materialized conception satisfy the
imagination of the reader of this book, an imagination that has
been stimulated by Hilton's words to producing for itself
something of delicate and fairy loveliness ?

Moderation as a philosophy has its appeal. Its virtues cannot be taught ; they must be experienced to be appreciated.
It is perhaps the philosophy of maturity rather than youth,
though the wise youth could know and savor it. Moderation
in food and drink, moderation in love and hate, moderation in
enthusiasm and in despair, it all leads to satisfaction without
satiety. Mr. Stimson, the Ambassador, told me that he had
recognized me at once in Buenos Aires. He had attended a
Yale-Harvard football game in my Senior year. Yale had won
and he had seen me leave the grounds with a group of friends.
He said my face remained in his memory as the happiest he
had ever seen, the joy of victory was bursting from me. Yet

I can't remember that episode while I remember so vividly a hundred later joys when I had learned to savor them with moderation. Without moderation no pleasure can be really enduring, a self-restraint in tasting will add a pungency to any flavor. Moderation even robs the bad of most of its evil. I don't say that you could become a moderate thief or murderer, but you could perhaps, without fear of grave consequences, covet your neighbor's wife, in moderation.

The great flow of war-time trade had begun to set in, the farmers and packers of the Argentine were beginning to flourish. There had been something approaching stagnation the first months of the war, trade had been dislocated, credits had to be re-established, shipping had to return to normal routes. Above all the menace to trade of German raiders had to be eliminated, otherwise freight and insurance rates were prohibitive. A naval war ensued in South American waters which passed almost unnoticed in the great struggle on the Continent but was of primary importance to the man on the street in Buenos Aires and directly affected his day-by-day existence. Admiral von Spee brought the German Asiatic squadron across the Pacific and suddenly appeared in Chilean waters. Craddock immediately set out from the vicinity of the Falklands with the British ships at his disposition, manifestly inferior to the German fleet. He seems to have been heroic and foolhardy when he engaged the Germans near Coronel in Chile. Craddock was killed, as was his crew, to a man ; his ships were sunk or dispersed. The battle of Coronel took place on November 1, 1914, and only a little more than a month later the tables were turned. Two British battle cruisers, mounting heavier metal than any of the Germans and of greater speed,

were dispatched to the Falkland Islands where they united
the remnants of the British naval power in those waters and
awaited the Germans. Admiral Sturdee lay in harbor until
the Germans were close at hand, sallied out and destroyed
them with the exception of the cruiser *Dresden*. The *Dresden* hid among the archipelago of the Straits of Magellan
and South Chile and for some time eluded capture or destruction.

Some months later a young American came into my office
and told me that late in December 1914 he had been running
a survey line among the barren hills of Tierra del Fuego, north
of the Straits of Magellan and that he had camped near the
summit of a hill of considerable size overlooking the Straits.
Directly below him was a small island, a narrow channel only
separating it from the mainland. Early one morning he saw
to his surprise a cruiser lying at anchor in this narrow channel,
its fires out, invisible from the Strait itself. Through his glasses
he identified the *Dresden*. As the day wore on three British
cruisers passed through the Strait, undoubtedly searching for
the *Dresden*, passed her within less than a mile, entirely unaware of her presence, and disappeared towards the Pacific.

As I read the history of those first two years of war and as
I think of the problems with which the Argentine Government
was struggling with both the British and French on the one
hand and the Germans on the other, I am struck with the similarity of the problems raised for neutrals and by the fact that
so little effort was made to harmonize the policy of the great
producing neutral states. All the Foreign Offices were excessively busy, but they took up their problems one by one with
the individual belligerents, and it does not seem to have oc-

curred to us or the other exporting neutrals that if we had united in the insistence on certain rights for trade or on certain consideration for our citizens, we would have possessed an immense economic weight. It was only during the last Pan-American meeting in Buenos Aires that the idea was seriously urged by Mr. Cordell Hull, Chief of the American Delegation. The idea of harmonizing the policy of neutrals awakened wide interest throughout the world, but it was not considered practical at Buenos Aires to make a tangible advance. There might, of course, be something antagonistic between such harmonization and the obligations of States members of the League of Nations. However, in the evolution that the League is undergoing it may be that the obligations of members will be reduced or, at least, more clearly specified ; in that event we may again be able to discuss a co-ordinated neutral policy. The idea might be of real interest and it may even prove to be of immense advantage for a number of States to act together to preserve an ordered existence governed by ad-mitted law and not by expediency only in a period when a por-tion of the world is in conflagration.

The rush of prosperity set in and was immense when it came, but it didn't come fast enough in all cases to save business, par-ticularly luxury concerns accustomed to long term credit and slow turnover. Jewellers were particularly badly hit, and the famous house of 'Catts' on the Calle Florida went into bankruptcy. The creditors arranged an auction ; naturally my wife, as every other woman in Buenos Aires, was in a state of excitement. We marked down two rings and fixed in our minds maximum amounts that we would pay for them. When the first ring was put up to auction I soon found myself bidding against one voice only from the far side of the room. As the price approached my maximum, I began to realize there was something familiar about that voice, left Kate to continue the bids while I hurried over to investigate. I found George Lorillard bidding against us, both of us unaware who our opponents were, and both indignant at finding the other. We quickly patched up a modus vivendi and separated the objects of our desire. There was also an auction of the effects of a picture dealer who had collapsed. We bought some pictures too — mentally — but mentally only. I remember that the lowest opening bid greatly exceeded the maxima that we had fixed. At least we must have had good taste.

I don't think that I was a very good Secretary of Embassy at Buenos Aires. I have subsequently looked up my record for this period in the Personnel Section of the Department of State and find no particular criticism of my work or attitude. Nevertheless as I look back on it I am far from satisfied. I never identified myself sufficiently with the place, I never convinced myself sufficiently that there was really useful work to be done or that I was doing it. Several factors unsettled me. The first was that I had seen Spanish civilization in its more primitive, and to me, more likable form in Central America. I had been imbued with that civilization as it was when it dreamed through the centuries between the coming of Cortez and Pizarro, to the beginning of the Nineteenth Century. To see it applied to something new and bold as my own city of Chicago seemed to me somewhat misplaced. Also the war was a constant reminder that we were working at something infinitely removed from the history that was being made in Europe. There the future of our civilization, the whole of our world, was in play ; whatever the end of the war it could not fail to affect our future life. We were neutrals but it became increasingly clear to me that the fate of the United States depended on the outcome of this war. It would never be quite the same United States again, but it would alter less if France and Great Britain came out victorious. Change was inevitable through the enormous industrial expansion we were making, but a victory for the Allies meant, to my thinking, a modification of social relations and not a transformation in the spirit of our institutions. If Germany were victorious, I feared a change in our country which would, of necessity, be fundamental to meet different conceptions of human relationships. For the first time I began to wish that I might have a voice in our destiny. It seemed increasingly unsatisfactory to be leading my daily life among incidents which had only remote interest to us while events of passionate interest were taking place in the world.

There was another and more intimate reason why I question the value of the work I did in Buenos Aires. My wife went through a desperate illness. For months she had been on a diet so rigorous that she used to come to the table with me and watch me eat with wistful intentness. If I left so much as a stalk of asparagus she would burst into tears at the thought of the waste. At last there came a period when I was not allowed to see her, and it was Mrs. Stimson who came and told me that our little boy had been born — dead. After weeks of apathy, my wife slowly recovered, and we drove out to the Chacarita Cemetery for her to see a little stone slab carved very simply, 'In Memory of our Son.'

The Doctor was dissatisfied with the slow recovery my wife

was making. We sought a change and visited Mar del Plata where the Ambassador had taken a cottage but she seemed unable to shake off her weakness. Eventually the Doctor ordered me to take her home, let her see her family ; he feared she would not otherwise recover. I applied for leave and obtained it. We decided to return by way of the West Coast and the Panama Canal, both because there was still talk of raiders in the Atlantic, and because we had never seen that part of the world. I wanted to go from Chile to La Paz and see a city built on the roof of the world, cross Lake Titicaca and reach Lima by way of Cusco. Pictures of the Inca ruins there had stirred my interest. But the Doctor vetoed any such expedition. He said it was folly for my wife to make it so we had to give it up. The American Delegation to the Financial Conference was leaving about that time and Mrs. McAdoo invited us to travel with them as far as Santiago de Chile. We gratefully accepted.

The first stage of our homeward journey took us from Buenos Aires to Mendoza at the foot of the Cordillera. We travelled over the vast plain of Argentina. It is incredibly big, the plain, and is broken by only one stretch of hills, one patch in which the scenery varies from its flat monotony. It had been raining heavily and portions of the plains were inundated. I was surprised at the quantity of wild fowl that arose from the pools and hurried away at the approach of the train. Long-legged cranes stood their ground, however, and watched us incuriously. I have never had the same impression of endless space, not even in crossing Kansas and Nebraska.

Mr. McAdoo had been so busy in the Conference that up to

this moment I had seen little of him, his time had been taken
up fully with the exalted of Latin America.   Crossing the wide
plains of the Argentine, however, was a different sort of life.
We sat for hours at a stretch on the back platform, Mr. Mc-
Adoo with his long legs stretched out, his flashing smile in
evidence, yarning incessantly.   We laughed until our sides
ached : two more amusing people than Mr. McAdoo and his
wife would be hard to find.

As far as I knew I was not leaving the Argentine definitely.
At the end of my leave I fully expected to return.   Our flat
was still furnished ; we had merely turned the key and walked
out.   Nevertheless I had a feeling of relief in leaving Buenos
Aires.   I had never become deeply interested either in the
country or its political life.   The flatness and dullness of the
country with its one huge sophisticated city failed to stimu-
late the imagination.   In colonial days it was the most remote
district of the Captaincy-General of Peru and its history, with
few exceptions, was strictly internal and full of local combats.
It seemed to me that even in the beginning of the Twentieth
Century its political life was still colored by these limitations.
However passionate the interest of the participant in local
strife, it does not interest the foreigner unless the rival forces
seem to be fighting for something other than office.   The de-
bates in the Chamber, the articles in the newspapers, the political argument one heard in the Clubs or on the street dealt
with personalities and not with national problems.   After a
year and a half of residence I should have been hard put to
it to define the conflicting political principles of the President
of the Republic and the leader of the opposition party.   I
imagine this is much less true today ; I read of party struggle

along social and international political lines, I read of vigorous international effort by the Minister for Foreign Affairs. Then, however, it impressed me as of little interest to the foreign observer.

The city was not Spanish though it sprang from a Spanish stock, and its inhabitants were deeply under the influence of Spanish history and culture ; it was not French in spite of its Parisian façades and Parisian shop windows ; it was certainly not English in spite of its Jockey Club and race tracks. Nor was it indigenous ; it was too unlike anything that I saw in the rest of the country to have sprung from the soil, and too reminiscent of other civilizations to be original. The failure to become interested in it and gain an affection for it is probably my fault and not the city's. I have encountered many Americans, both travellers and diplomats, who assure me that my impression is erroneous.

Nothing is more illusive than the quality of being sympathetic, nothing is harder to seize than the reasons why a place or a person makes an especial appeal to you. However extravert you may be, the state of your own mind colors that place or that person in your memory and in your experience, and my mind at that time, as I have described, was colored by other preoccupations than the country in which I was living.

The train pulled into Mendoza at the foot of the Andes where you change from the broad-gauge to the mountain railway. The Mayor gave us samples of his Mendoza wines. They were light and pleasant and will probably have a future as the climate is splendidly adapted to vine culture. I had done the trip before with Colonel Brainard, but I was as absorbed as the others by the scenery of that stupendous climb.

Some of the travellers suffered from the altitude ; they even had to bring out the emergency oxygen tank to revive Senator Fletcher. The train halts before it enters the final tunnel. We got out but were breathless with a walk down the platform. The train puffed through the tunnel, slid silently into the down grade, came into blazing sunlight pouring over the lovely plain of Chile below.

CHAPTER XI

Boats from Chile were hard to come by in those days. It was harder still to get cabins on them when they did run, such was the rush of those wanting to travel and to ship on the little available space. We considered ourselves lucky to have obtained a cabin on a Norwegian freighter from Valparaiso to Cristóbal on the eastern end of the Panama Canal. Our feeling of satisfaction, however, lasted only until we saw the boat and the cabin. The boat was so laden that it bucked every wave, water ran over the decks even on days of calm swell. Cargo was stacked on the deck so that you tore your breeches on nails as you tried to walk around. A number of cattle were in the bow. They smelled pretty high and became higher as we neared the Equator. In the cabin were two bunks and nothing else. I mean nothing else in the way of accommodations — there were plenty of cockroaches and spiders. No place to leave anything ; we never unpacked and wore the same clothes the entire trip.

I enjoyed that trip nevertheless. Kate's health improved rapidly, the change of scene was obviously doing her good. We landed at many odd places that the big boats do not touch. We loaded and unloaded freight at Antofagasta, Iquique, Arica, Mollendo, besides the normal ports of call, Callao and Guayaquil. Even without wind the swell of the Pacific is heavy in those southern waters, and as there are practically no harbors from Valparaiso to Callao, the boat at anchor was not only hot but uncomfortable and noisy. So we always went ashore, going down the swaying ladder into a barge or being slung in a basket by a crane and deposited with a thump. I have few definite recollections of most of those places but remember a restaurant at Mollendo built out over the surf where we ate the queerest sort of sea-food while the building shook with every wave and you had to shout to make yourself heard over the roar.

We must have had a heavy cargo to take on at Arica because there was time to take a train and spend a day at Tacna. My wife and I sat in the main square of the town, the church bells chimed the noon hour, everybody was at lunch and not a man or a woman, not a dog or a cat, was visible. Tacna seemed on another planet though it was only some fifty miles from the coast. I looked at the faraway mountains, the desert broken here and there with patches of green cultivation, the lonely plaza where I sat, and wondered at the intensity of the struggle which had gone on about this apparently useless region. Ever since the war in my childhood Chile and Peru had been hostile because of this strip of land while Bolivia watched them both with jealous eyes. After the Great War and during and after the period of the plebiscite, there were years of bloodshed and intimidation before this 'American Alsace-Lorraine' question was finally settled. That it was finally settled without a further war is an encouraging evidence of the solubility by peaceful means of nearly all thorny questions, given a measure of good-will and peaceful intent.

We spent a couple of days in Lima, while the ship lay in Callao. In Lima I was home again. Here was the Latin America that I knew, that I had come to appreciate in Guatemala.

Beamed and plastered houses with lovely carved wood work on balcony and doors, glimpses of patios with flowers and fountains. A sense of time elapsed, an indifference to the present, a sort of haughty ignoring of the life of the modern world. In colonial days Lima was the capital of most of South America, its Viceroy ruled at least theoretically as far as Patagonia and over the Andes in Colombia and Venezuela. Communication was incredibly slow and the hand of the Viceroy on the local governors must have been lightly felt. Nevertheless, the great Empire gave to Lima a dignity and formality of an Empire centre. They say that the climate is unspeakably dreary, with its damp grey Pacific mists and that you come to long for sunshine as a blessing beyond price. But it was satisfying to me.

We barely touched Guayaquil, the crew had hardly begun to take on cargo when word reached the Captain that yellow fever had been reported. He hastily recalled his crew, abandoned the cargo, and put to sea.

Since the day when Balboa, led by Indian tales of a great sea to the west, first drove his little band of men through the forests and swamps of Panama to look upon the Pacific Ocean, Panama has been the spot in the American hemisphere fullest of romance and swashbuckling adventure. Its history is packed like a Gobelin tapestry with color, riches, battle, and plunder. Here Pizarro built and fitted out his fleet for the conquest of the Incas. Drake harried the towns and looted the treasure trains. Sir Henry Morgan, most magnificent of freebooters, led his band of brigands across the marshes and green rivers to loot the city. It was over Panama that the Viceroys and Captains-General, clad in armor inlaid with silver and accompanied by pageantry of Church and State, re-shipped to the capital city of Lima.   They landed at Panama the loot of gold and silver from the Inca treasure and the Inca mines, they carried it over the Isthmus and reshipped it in Spanish galleons that had to run the gauntlet of privateers and pirates of all nations.   Miners and adventurers pushed breath-less across the narrow strip in 1849 to share in the gold of California, many of them to die of yellow fever on the West Coast unable to find or pay for transport north.   Finally, the greatest romance of all, modern Americans have built a water-way over hill and valley, through lake and mountain range, where the greatest ships can pass to the far ends of the earth and avoid the long and stormy haul around the Cape of Good Hope or through the Straits of Magellan.

It is a stirring thing, the Panama Canal ; it stimulates the imagination as does the Suez, but it has a quality the Suez lacks — amazing beauty.   If we listed our marvels in modern times, it would be one of the 'Seven Wonders of the World.'   It gives the impression of might and power, clothed in beauty. The results of might and power are there, great ships rise and sink in the locks ; they move in stately fashion, towed by tiny electric motors, a great feat of engineering in a setting of jungle and flowers and sun on green slopes.   After sunset the ship came to the top of the eastern locks, sudden darkness fell, the locks were illuminated like a gigantic flight of steps twinkling below you, the city of Cristóbal lighted the edge of the sea, a space of blackness separating the lights of man from the bril-liant stars of the tropics.

It was a memorable day for me, the passage of the Panama Canal.   This was the work of my countrymen, Americans had had the daring to believe that an area of death could be made safe for men to work. Americans had dreamed and carried out the mighty engineering feat. Americans had kept it all beautiful. I was proud of being American.

The yellow fever scare had been reported from Guayaquil so we were not permitted to land either in Panama or Colon on the west nor in Cristóbal on the east coast. Indeed the health authorities held us aboard our ship in quarantine for several days tied to a wharf in the blazing sun of Cristóbal. One day we heard a voice from the wharf loudly demanding Kate and Hugh Wilson. It was Kermit Roosevelt. He explained by shouting up to us as we leaned over the rail that though they should have reached New York by now, Belle had fallen ill and they had been obliged to break the voyage to take her to a hospital there. In the meantime, the rest of the ship's passengers, welcoming any diversion in the boredom of being tied to the dock, had come to the rail and were listening and becoming more and more interested in the conversation, all carried on at the top of our lungs. Now Kermit has a complete unawareness of any fact in the world except the one on which he happens to be concentrating. It is not that he is contemptuous of what people are thinking about him : it is simply that he doesn't know they exist. The following bellowed conversation ensued : *Kermit* — 'Belle was getting better but had a relapse.' *Kate*, self and passengers all hanging over the rail — 'What rotten luck.' *Kermit* — 'She threw up.' *Passengers* — 'How awful.' 'Three times,' bawled Kermit.

At last we were declared free of danger of fever and permitted to cross the wharf and board a boat flying the American flag of the United Fruit Company. She set out for New

York.   In the hundreds of sea voyages I have made in my life, none has been so much appreciated.   The contrast between the ship we had left and our present boat was heaven.   The cleanliness, the space, the coolness, the good food, how you love them when you have been deprived of them !   When things are primitive, you don't feel any particular hardship or deprivation when you are without the material things that we consider essential to civilization.   But when conditions are not primitive but are dirty and disagreeable we feel a resentment and disgust.   That must be why the relief of boarding the American vessel stays so vividly in my memory.

New York presented its usual bewildering changes.   I can never return to that city without becoming a tourist and embarking on an expedition to see what new miracles of architecture New York has achieved or what new adventures New York has embarked upon.   Landing there is inevitably stimulating and exciting.   This landing was no exception, but I shall leave descriptions of arrivals in New York to foreigners who experience even more excitement than I and who come to the adventure with, perhaps, a fresher palate.

Friends of ours in New York talked enthusiastically about a film called 'The Birth of a Nation' so we went to see it.   It was a sight to revolutionize my conception of the cinema. Here I found drama, history, coupled with an art of presentation which changed the cinema from a mere distraction to something which could compete with the stage in the presentation of dramatic art.   Since that day I have been, I confess with pride, a devotee of the movies.   I have watched with the greatest interest its development ; the institution of the talkie, the serious endeavor to present great pieces to the public. Here was a presentation which need not be confined to the great capitals of the world but could be shown in small towns, at a reasonable price, to the people of every country. I have lived too much of my life in small places not to appreciate what an extraordinary boon the movies would become and have become to the great mass of mankind who must think of their expenditure and yet wish to satisfy an appetite for beautiful things. Only the other day I saw 'Romeo and Juliet' in the cinema. I don't believe that any stage production of this tragedy has been so comprehensive, so well acted by the subordinate characters nor, above all, so well spoken by all the cast, as in this recent film. Indeed, since the introduction of the talkies, it has been interesting to note the gradual and impressive improvement not only of cinema technique but of the spoken word. The repercussions have been far-reaching. I have even noted a corresponding improvement in the spoken word, particularly among women, as I return to the United States. The despised cinema has been of extraordinary educational value to our nation, and every shop girl is trying to model her voice on that of her favorite in the movies. 'The Birth of a Nation' marked the beginning of the new trend and was the conception of someone with great artistic imagination. He should receive due tribute for it.

Happily my vacation coincided with the tenth reunion of my class at Yale in New Haven. I had the satisfaction of finding that the men in my class looked exactly the same as at graduation, and of being told that I myself did. The satisfaction took wing when I was introduced to a group of graduating Seniors at Mory's and found them so youthful in appearance that I was shocked. I have noticed the same phenomenon each time I have gone to reunion : one's contemporaries do not seem to change, they have to be compared to their own sons or to their graduating pictures to bring home a realization of time's grisly changes.

This visit to New Haven was the last time I saw the University as I had known it, for by the time of my next visit the Harkness and Stirling gifts had changed it almost beyond recognition. I felt rather resentful of all the change until in June of 1936 I made a tour of the University, talked to the Professors and began to understand the purpose. Also some of the buildings were highly successful. I did not much like the construction of Gothic style ; it seemed a too conscious imitation of Oxford and Cambridge and had no particular excuse for existence in an American seat of learning. Nevertheless I did contemplate with genuine pleasure construction which was native to our soil, a sort of New England Georgian architecture which has been adapted for modern use, for instance, the Divinity School and Timothy Dwight College. These buildings belong to America, they are part of our history and carry the American tradition into the lives of the young men who live there. Incidentally, I can think of no surroundings in which it would be more agreeable to pass one's life than those of the Master of one of the Colleges. Certainly in the rush of life in the United States, it must be reassuring and comforting to be able to look out upon the Courts of Timothy Dwight or Davenport.

In the midst of our reunion came the mobilization of the National Guard to the Mexican frontier. Several of my classmates had to pack up hastily and depart. The country did not seem deeply interested ; they hardly realized the risk they were running of a first class war. We have only to suppose, for instance, that Pershing's expedition had encountered real resistance, that Villa had been aided by the Central Government and that our expedition had met with a defeat with heavy loss of life. In all probability the country would have blazed into a war fever, demanded revenge, and a real war with Mexico would have been under way. It is interesting to contemplate historical 'might have beens.' If we had had a war with Mexico to deal with it is unlikely that we would have entered the great war less than a year later. The consequences are incalculable, but surely Europe today would be very different from what it is, and the map of North America as well might show very different frontiers. Accident in history is one of the most potent factors, and the ruler of a country can never know at what moment he is making a decision that will prove an historical cross-road. Among the portentous decisions in history, surely Mr. Wilson's recall of Pershing from further pursuit of his objective in Mexico stands among the most important.

The *Lusitania* had been sunk, scores of notes had been written. Among my friends both in the East and in Chicago there was widespread indignation and a demand to adopt a more vigorous, attitude towards Germany even at the risk of war. Nevertheless I had the impression that the mass of the nation was satisfied with the Administration's policy. Industry was roaring, agricultural products were high, everybody was making money and labor was well employed at good wages. I certainly adopted at this time the comfortable belief that Germany would not make our neutrality impossible by the commission of acts which would drive us, even against our inclination, into the war. There were few people, it seemed to me, really desirous that we should immediately plunge in on the side of the Allies. Mr. Theodore Roosevelt was certainly active, but while my friends applauded his sentiments of anger and condemnation of Germany, they halted at the point of advocating a rupture of relations with that country. There was still a certain amount of hostility to Great Britain because of the Orders in Council in respect to trade with the Netherlands and the Scandinavian countries. Curiously there was nothing but sympathy for France ; interference of our trade by France was not even mentioned.

In Chicago our business was sharing in the general well-being. My brother took me to the Commercial Club and other gatherings of business men where political debate became hot. I noticed among these men and even among my father's friends a more tolerant attitude towards my profession than they had shown six years before when I had talked it over with them. Their tolerance in some cases even reached the point of sympathetic interest. They had been deeply stirred by foreign events in the past two years. They had learned a lot of policy, some geography and even traces of history. They became indignant over Japan's seizure of Shantung and knew where Shantung was, they had been obliged to learn about Poland, Galicia, and Rumania to follow events on the eastern front. Some of them even followed events on the Salonika front and could distinguish the Balkan countries instead of grouping them all under the comprehensive word 'Bohunks.'

And as they learned geography and as they recognized our own country's interest in alien events, so their interest grew in a service which was destined to administer our interests and look out for them. There has never been any question in my mind since that visit ; the business men of America believe in the Foreign Service, or will believe in it when they are told about it. A trained service represents to their minds the normal and logical way of going about the nation's business. It is what they would do for their own concerns. Why should Uncle Sam do differently ? Certain of the American companies have built up their own foreign services ; the Standard Oil has a graded service of foreign representatives. So the business men instinctively accept the idea of a trained service for the State Department.

The change in their attitude came just about the time of which I am writing. Before the war America exported raw materials only. Speaking generally, raw materials do not need salesmanship ; price quotation on specified grade is usually sufficient. During the war, however, we began to ship manufactured articles, and these encounter real competition where salesmanship and full knowledge of the field is required. Also we began to ship credit, if you can use the expression, and our investments abroad needed all the knowledge and protection they could get. The realization of these factors has brought our business men from indifference to real interest in the Foreign Service. The process was just beginning in 1916.

I was about to play in a four-ball foursome from the first tee at Wheaton near Chicago when a messenger ran from the Club House with a telegram in his hand. I tore it open. 'You are transferred to Berlin as Second Secretary. Mr. Joseph Grew, Counselor at Berlin, will communicate with you as to departure. (*signed*) Bryan,' is about the way it read. It was tremendous. I think in all the vicissitudes of diplomatic existence no official message has at the same time so delighted me and so upset me. It meant going into the heart of things. It meant work of deep interest. It meant excitement, adventure. Berlin was then the centre of a great fortress. The Allies were hammering on the West, on the East, on the South at Salonika and on the Alps. Very little authentic news came from Central Europe ; to go there was to plunge into the unknown. The terrific bombardment and attack on Verdun was just dying down, a sullen muttering of the guns continued, but it seemed as if the attack had failed, while rumors were current of preparation by the Allies of a mass drive on the Somme.

And how would my wife take it ? Would she like the idea of this venture or would she regret all the things she would have to abandon in Buenos Aires ? These thoughts whirled about in my mind. I played a vile game and the foursome cost me seven dollars. As soon as it was over I sent a telegram to my wife who was visiting her family where the experience was doing her all the good the Argentine doctor had prophesied. I wrote, 'Transferred to Berlin. Don't burst into tears until I can talk to you about it. Coming by first train.' But I had no need to worry. Kate had adopted the diplomatic service and was as excited as I was. She already knew Berlin, having studied music there for a couple of years some time before. So we dispatched a cable to Buenos Aires to sell at auction everything we owned and started our preparations for the new post.

A telegram came from Joseph Grew asking me to stop in Boston on my way to Washington to discuss plans. I agreed and that visit began for me a close friendship which still endures. Joe Grew is now Ambassador to Tokyo. He has made one of the finest records in our Service, among other posts Minister to Switzerland, Under Secretary of State, Ambassador to Turkey. He has never been in politics, his service record only has been his backing. He is one of the oldest members in point of view of years of service, and I have never heard the rightness of one of his appointments questioned. He is tall, slender, and distinguished-looking, with black moustache and heavy eyebrows. He has great charm of manner and earns friendship and trust wherever he is sent. His reports are scholarly and able and his judgment sound and unflurried by excitement. Joe had left his wife, Alice, and his little girls in Europe, so I did not meet them until we reached Berlin. Alice and my wife quickly became close friends and have so remained. Alice had gleaming black hair, a flashing smile, a slender and beautifully clothed figure. She was a most indefatigable hostess, full of humor, at her best when the humor was at her own expense.

Joe told me that the Second Secretary at Berlin had just died there and that the Ambassador had cabled him to pick a man to fill the place ; that after discussing the affair with William Phillips they had selected me. He added that he had been happy to note on my record that I knew some German. I was overcome with embarrassment and had to confess that when I had come to the Department for my examination I had been interviewed by one of the men in the Personnel Section. This chap had asked me if I knew any other language than French and I had replied in the negative. He then said that I would be examined in one language only, but if I had even studied any other, it was well to put it down. 'Well,' said I, 'up to the time I was seven years old we had a German governess in the house, and I spoke baby German which I have since forgotten.' 'Right,' said he, 'we'll put it down.' This had gone out of my mind completely until Joe spoke. I was highly chagrined, but at least the episode made me study German desperately when I got to Berlin and in a few months I could see my way through my daily business at the office. He said he planned to sail in June on the *St. Paul*, spend a few days in London, thence to Berlin over the Hook of Holland, and suggested we go together. This suited me admirably, and I took passage with him.

Saying good-bye to our friends for that expedition made me realize in some slight degree what the departure of the early explorers must have been like. I imagine that when Magellan left Lisbon to sail around the world and his friends came to bring gifts and see him off, they made hearty jokes and wished him good luck, then turned away with a sigh and thought, 'That's the last of *him*.' Such were the tales of atrocities and frightfulness in Germany that I know our friends had grave doubts of seeing us again. Anyway they brought gifts. Now in my experience an ocean voyage is one long struggle to prevent yourself from eating twice as much as you need. You have breakfast, usually hearty ; at eleven in the morning they give you hot soup hoping you can live on that until lunch at one. At 4 :30 comes tea with immense slabs of raisin cake, then dinner at eight and, lest you should be faint in the evening, sandwiches at 11:00 p.m. in the smoke-room. In spite of this regime, and all your friends know it as well as you do, they continue to send great boxes of food, fruit and sweets, and you never know what to do with them. On this occasion Kate made up a great basket of some of our supplies and sent me to deliver it to Joe in case he was suffering from hunger. I started out of the cabin and bumped into Joe just coming to deliver a similar gift to us. I suppose the habit of sending food comes from the days when there was no refrigeration so the fresh things spoiled after the first week and the traveller finished the trip on salt pork and ship's biscuits. The gifts are now an anachronism, and I would rather have the money instead.

I am glad the old *St. Paul* is no longer crossing the Atlantic. She was uncomfortable to a degree that must have been experienced to be believed. We had a suite on the promenade deck. It had nude figures molded in the plaster, but the seats and sofa were of shiny black leather, and you slid to the floor when the boat rolled. The voyage was uneventful, though as we approached the British Isles there was some apprehension of submarines. There was a great American flag painted on both sides of the bow and flood-lighted at night, but you could not be sure that the commander of a submarine might not shoot first and look at the flag afterwards. We got off at Liverpool with real relief and came on to London.

Joe had a lot of business to do in London so we waited there several days. London was in an optimistic mood. The Battle of Jutland had been recently fought and, whatever subsequent historians may have written about that conflict, to the British public it had been presented as a victory, and the people were correspondingly elated. British supremacy of the sea had been reasserted, and the German fleet had been driven back into its harbors. Whispers went around of the tremendous push that was being prepared for that summer, an effort of such magnitude that it could not be resisted. The Battle of the Somme was in preparation.

I roamed the streets, watched soldiers being drilled in Hyde Park and Green Park, saw recruits being put through setting-up drill clad in bowlers and caps. The city had changed less in appearance than I had supposed, the streets seemed perhaps a trifle quieter, but there was little sign of war-time activity. A few soldiers walked about, and the restaurants and theatres showed a number of officers decorously enjoying their leave. Later I encountered officers on leave in Paris, officers of all kinds of armies, and their enjoyment of their brief holiday was anything but decorous. Not so in London, however. There wasn't even much talk of the war. I was told by my friends that 'business as usual' had been adopted as a slogan and was being followed literally. I got the impression of an ordered and restrained determination. I did not know London at all at that time so I had no way of penetrating the heart and mind of the people. It was only years later, in fact, in the Naval Conference of 1930 that I began to appreciate it and to understand something of it. Just as Paris is the city of youth, so London is the city of maturity, its fine flavor can appeal best to a seasoned palate.

We sailed at midnight from Tilbury. When we awoke in the morning we were quietly at anchor still in the mouth of the Thames ; orders had been received from the Admiralty to await further instructions. A light, slowly moving bank of fog enveloped us. Suddenly two destroyers broke through the fog, coming at top speed, dense black smoke pouring from their four funnels. They circled us still at high speed, wig-wagged a message and disappeared into the North Sea. We hauled up anchor and followed them. The trip to the Hook is not long, but at that time it was full of emotion. You had to keep your life-belts handy, even on deck we carried them with us. For no apparent reason the boat would slow down, deviate in wide circles and continue its course. We reached The Hague without incident.

On the train to Berlin I took stock of my situation. I was going to a new field. I had travelled a bit in Central Europe but knew next to nothing about it. I knew that I would be given work in the Embassy of a non-political nature ; I was not competent to handle anything else. The thing for me to do, I decided, was to work with all there was in me, not only to do my job competently, whatever it might be, but to learn about the situation as soon as possible to make myself capable of doing more interesting work. I wanted to begin on that sort of diplomacy that I knew was being carried on, but that I had never been called upon to do. I knew it would be a large order as the routine would doubtless be a full task in itself, but that the result would be worth the effort, I felt sure.

CHAPTER XII

The Embassy at Berlin and the Chancery as well were housed in a rented building at 7 Wilhelmplatz. The situation was excellent as we had only to cross the square and the Wilhelmstrasse to reach the Foreign Office and that of the Chancellor. Mr. James Gerard was the Ambassador. He is well known to the American public and to the British public also, since he has just served as the President's special representative at the Coronation of King George VI. He was young, vigorous and forceful, his moral courage was of a high order, he spoke without intimidation to the highest in the land and urged the point of view of the United States with the same vigor on the Kaiser and on the lowliest member of the Foreign Office. He was a much better Ambassador, I always feel, than his own book makes him out to be. The pity of it was he was not always properly supported by the State Department so that the full results of his vigorous activity could not make themselves felt. Again and again the force of his presentation of America's case was mitigated by soothing words from the Department, duly reported to Berlin by Ambassador Bernstorff.

In conversation Mr. Gerard was humorous and caustic ; he had an impish delight in creating embarrassing situations. His joy was apparent when he had at his table American women married to Germans, whom he would tease until they were on the verge of tears. He accepted as good as he gave ; if the object of his particular attack could answer back and turn the tables on him he was delighted. His staff did not escape embarrassment. The first time I lunched with them he called down the table to me, 'You say you don't speak German but do speak French and Spanish. What is the word for a tin-can in both languages ?' We all loved Mrs. Gerard, a gracious figure with prematurely grey hair. She went out of her way to be kind and was a hostess and Ambassadress of whom we were all proud. Her hospitality was unlimited and there was nothing demanding about her. She needed to be a personality because she had to deal with a lot of strong personalities among the women of the staff. She carried it off beautifully.

The Embassy staff was a little world in itself. The situation in Berlin drove us in upon ourselves, threw us into unusual intimacy and brought it about that our relations with the Germans were nearly all on official footing. Long before my arrival the Germans had realized the hostility of American public opinion. They were under no illusions about our sentiments ; they still hoped that we might be kept from active participation in the war. Certainly, however, we were potential enemies. There was little social life in Berlin anyway during this period, but what little there was we did not share — there was too wide a gap between our thoughts and theirs to make social relations agreeable or even possible. Far better not to risk it. For the same reason we rarely went to the theatres, or if we did, kept still during the intermissions lest the sound of a conversation in English give rise to unpleasantness. In restaurants we either took private rooms or went to those places like Hillers where they were accustomed to foreigners. Concerts we could and did attend ; they were just as lovely during those war days as they always are in Berlin. For the most part, however, we found our amusement among ourselves. We were numerous enough, young enough and, we thought, attractive enough to divert ourselves through our own devices. I confess that amusement played a large part in our lives during those months. We were working at feverish activity — frequently our evenings would be interrupted by a call to the Chancery — we were living among a people hostile to us, maintaining a faith and a hope the antithesis to ours, our working hours were full of cases and tales of misery and suffering, we sought eagerly the anodyne of gaiety in our free time.

I do not mean to say that we saw no Germans ; of course we saw numbers of them in official life, as well as old friends that we might happen to have known, but they took little part in the intimate life of the staff. But there were a number of American women married to Germans whom we saw constantly. Princess Isenburg, Baroness Speck von Sternburg and others came often to our houses, while Edith von Kleist and Gertie von Bocklin were almost members of the staff. These two sisters were full of charm and gaiety and are among our pleasantest memories of the city. Travellers came on occasion, but rarely. William Bullitt, now Ambassador to Paris, visited Berlin, I believe as a newspaper correspondent. He held us convulsed with his fantastic account of Mr. Ford's Peace Ship with its curious cargo of humanity.

Among those whom we saw intimately and who, for reasons which follow, interested me particularly, were Mr. and Mrs. John Brinkerhoff Jackson. Mr. Jackson was in charge of the protection of prisoners of war of those nations, notably

Great Britain and Japan, whose governments had turned over their interests to the United States when they became belligerents. Jackson had had a long career in the American Foreign Service, a rather remarkable career in those days when even the Secretaries of Embassy were political appointments. A graduate of Annapolis, he had done considerable service in the Navy, obtained foreign appointments, among others about a dozen years as Counsellor of Embassy in Berlin, Minister in Rumania, Athens, and Havana.

Jackson had retired on the assumption of office of a Democratic President, but had offered his services and been taken on at Berlin when the war broke out. He was large and florid, blond hair parted in the middle and a long blond moustache with a similar parting. His wife, Auntie Jackie we called her, was equally large, not so tall, dressed as if she had stepped out of a bandbox. Jackson ate an enormous breakfast, no lunch, and a gargantuan dinner. They lived at the Esplanade Hotel, and I can see them now seated at a small table, invariably dressed in full dinner costume, two tall goblets in front of them with peeled peaches in the bottom, ready for a nightly bottle of champagne to be poured over them. The meal closed by eating the peach impregnated with champagne. It was a spectacle of satisfaction that always gave me pleasure in that grim city. The intimate acquaintance that Jackson had among soldiers and political men in Germany was of high advantage to him in this work with prisoners. If he visited a prisoners' camp it was probable that he was personally known to the commanding officer, at least they had mutual friends and memories. He was able to accomplish much for the prisoners' benefit through these personal relationships, perhaps more than he might have done by thumping the table and loudly demanding rights instead of asking favors. Neverthe- less, he was an unhappy man. Practically without exception, the staff of the American Embassy was persuaded that at some moment the Germans would make it impossible for the United States to stay out of the war, and that if we did come in under those circumstances, our entry would be righteous and for the benefit of civilization. To Jackson, the European conflict was a thing for Europe ; Germany was no more to blame than any other power, and the United States would be doing an iniquitous thing if it threw its weight on the side of the Al- lies. Relations were therefore not happy between Jackson and the Ambassador and other members of the staff, and the hostility of the staff was only tempered by the knowledge of the useful work that Jackson was doing and by the affection we all held for Auntie Jackie. When the United States en- tered the war Jackson moved to the Lake of Geneva, where he watched events and kept his mouth shut. I think I am the only man he talked to there ; he once burst out and told me that he was eating his heart out doing nothing while his country was fighting, but how could he take part in a war which he could only consider stupid and sinful, and based on lying reports of propaganda bureaus. So he stayed quietly in his hotel and died there a few years later. An unhappy man who could not see events with the eyes of his compatriots, but an honest and dignified man in his distress and disillusion. Auntie Jackie never moved away, and died quite recently in the same hotel on Lake Geneva.

There are so many of that sort of hotel in Switzerland. Among my early memories is that of being taken by my father and mother to Interlaken and to the Territet end of Lake Geneva. Then these hotels were in their heyday. Vast barrack-like constructions with huge ball and banquet rooms, they supplied a generation that had different tastes from ours. The gentlemen wore varnished button boots and spent the day seated in large chairs, in rocking-chairs, if they were American, looking at some famous view from the terrace, talking to the ladies and smoking cigars. In the evening they moved across the way to the Casino and had a bit of a flutter. Jackson and Auntie Jackie seemed to belong to this generation. This was the life they loved, they entertained solemnly at lavish meals and felt a heavy obligation of social responsibility. They were nearly the only guests in this vast establishment, and when you went to call on them your footsteps sounded loud and lonely in the deserted halls and corridors.

I have mentioned before that the concerts and other music in Berlin were as lovely as always during this period. In attending concerts and indeed in learning about them I was constantly thrown with Ellis Loring Dresel to whom music was a real passion. Dresel was in the section which dealt with the protection of prisoners of war. He was born in Boston, was a graduate of Harvard and of the Harvard Law School, had practised a bit of law in his life, but his main interest, until the war came, lay in bridge and polo. At the outbreak of the war, already a middle-aged man, he volunteered for service and was taken on by the Embassy in Berlin. His father had been a German, a musician of considerable merit, who had married a Boston woman. Ellis was so Boston that the very use of the word as an adjective now makes me think of him. His accent and way of life typified that city. Nevertheless, German was his second language, and he had inherited his father's love for and taste in music.

After a cheerful life in which Dresel had done little serious work, the war engrossed him, and he entered upon eight years of intense and useful work. His latent qualities became evident and were put to use. He showed calmness of judgment, persistence of effort, moral courage of a high order. His wisdom was profound and his diplomatic ability unusual. When we left Berlin, he stayed in Switzerland with me and became the representative in that country of the War Trade Board and of the American Red Cross while the United States was at war. Colonel House called him to Paris during the Peace Conference where he was the Head of the German Section in the American Delegation. The Conference terminated, he was sent to Berlin as American Commissioner where, in spite of the fact that the United States and Germany were still technically at war, he gained the confidence of the Germans to such an extent that they consulted him not only on foreign but also on their internal affairs. He negotiated the treaty of peace with Germany and remained at the post until an Ambassador was appointed in 1922. It was deplorable that a man of his talents and service was allowed to resign and that during the post-war years, when our need for skillful diplomacy was so crying, he was permitted to remain in disappointment and uselessness in his home in Boston. He had had a few years in which he exercised his talents, he knew that he was the master of them, and he died bitterly disappointed that he could not make use of them to the end.

There was a house where we often dropped in after work to drink a cocktail with Lanier and Aileen Winslow. A decrepit elevator accepted you on the ground floor, but whether or not it took you up rested on its own whim, and it was full of fancies. The apartment was always crowded, Aileen stood erect, young, pretty and slender, shaking cocktails in a shaker manufactured from a 4.7 shell. The baby Peter crawled about the floor in his pyjamas, ready for bed, and grinned and chuckled at the guests. Lanier, cocktail in hand, was telling some story that had his audience holding its sides. He was one of the best story tellers I have ever encountered, his language was pungent and full of wit, he had a rabelaisian gusto in life that never failed. It was an exuberant nature that found ground for laughter in everything, and he had the priceless gift of communicating his joy and his mirth in his salty speech. Lanier had his job to do in the Chancery, but I am convinced that his real job lay in keeping us all cheered up through some very grim months.

Lanier, as a good New Yorker, was a Democrat, so when election day came around, and the first reports came in of the victory of Mr. Hughes, Lanier paid off the bets that he had contracted. About dinner time, however, the news reached us that California had gone Democratic, giving the election to Mr. Wilson. Lanier immediately summoned the men with whom he had bet, and most of the rest of us as well, to dine at his house where the bets could be settled. What a dinner that was! Lanier told a tale that occurred through his having voted the Democratic ticket. Colonel House had taken Lanier with him to act as Private Secretary during one of his expeditions through Europe, and they were visiting the Embassy in Paris where Mr. Sharp was Ambassador. Lanier said that one day the Ambassador summoned him to his office, took special pains to see that all doors were shut, put both hands on Lanier's shoulders and whispered, 'Mr. Winslow, do you realize that there isn't another Democrat in my entire establishment!' Lanier died a few years ago, and I suffered a real loss. As you grow older you realize how much you owe to the men who have made you laugh, and how much affection is dependent upon jokes and humor shared in common. There are few men in the world with whom I have shared as much mirth as with Lanier.

The staff of the Embassy was so varied and so full of picturesque characters that I am tempted to dwell perhaps too long on them. There are several who, although unknown to the public, possessed characteristics and characters which leave them vividly in my mind. I will talk of one only. Mrs. Kirk, whom we all called Clara, was the mother of Margaret Ruddock, whose husband was a secretary in the staff, as well as of Alexander Kirk, another secretary. Both Albert and Alexander had been in the Ecole des Sciences Politique in Paris when I was a student there so that I knew them all intimately. Clara was as dear to me as a member of my family. She died a few months ago at an advanced age. She had led a vivid life. She retained her youthful decision, her vanities and her love of clothes, till the very end. She was a spicy conversationalist and feared neither man nor the devil. She loved youth and detested old men. We won't meet her like again. The brother and sister, Alexander and Margaret, were unlike in every respect save one — they both had strong wills ; and when their minds were made up it was difficult in the extreme to alter their decisions. Unlike as they were, they were equally positive and equally certain. Nevertheless, I have been present at several family councils ; Clara would listen to us all in complete placidity, then give her ruling in a few calm words, a ruling that was the essence of common sense. When that wise old woman had spoken, even the self-willed children in their full maturity would bow to her decision. Albert Ruddock had a different technique, he never argued, he was always placid, he merely did what he chose.

All of these people, at least the married portion of them, had houses or apartments in the same section of the city, between the Lutzow Canal and the Tiergarten, so we tried to find something in that area. Eventually we had a piece of luck, luck for us, bad luck for the owner. The owner of an apartment on the Lutzow Ufer, Mr. de Bestegui, Mexican Minister to Berlin, had married a Belgian woman before the war, and after remaining two years in Berlin while hostilities were being carried on, found the situation intolerable and moved to Brussels to stay with his wife's family. We took their flat and were delighted with it. It was a double-decker with an interior staircase, having the same drawback as all apartments in Berlin ; you had to go through the dining room and along the kitchen and pantry corridors to get to the sleeping accommodations. But the salons were well furnished, the dining room was gaily decorated to give cheer in a grey climate.

The downstairs was my domain. I had a library with a fireplace and big red leather chairs, a wide window looking on the Lutzow, where I could watch the barges go by, and a fencing room. We got hold of a boxing master and most of the Embassy, including the Ambassador, used to come to the house in the late afternoon for exercise. We had a bit of garden in the back ; although it was late September when we entered, we liked the garden so much that we furnished it with chairs, tables, and gaudy parasols which were all put away for the winter as soon as purchased and never seen again. Judge Gerard gave us entirely sound advice ; he said that the situation was too precarious for us to be taking leases on houses and 'spending money like drunken sailors,' that we ought to stay peacefully in the Hotel Esplanade and see how events shaped themselves in the next few months, which he rightly regarded as critical in our relations with Germany. But there are times when to be foolish is to be wise, and this was one of them ; we enjoyed that house, we loved having our friends in it and participating in the somewhat feverish gaiety of the Embassy staff.

Housekeeping presented a special problem. It was only with the greatest difficulty, at great expense, and in violation of the law, that anything except the most elementary food, black bread and cabbages, could be purchased in Berlin. Accordingly, the commissary, or grocery department, of the Embassy did a flourishing business. Every week orders were made up embodying the separate needs of the various households of the Embassy, forwarded to London and brought to Berlin by courier. The courier brought the supplies and mail from the Netherlands in a locked box-car ; he was a stout fellow, carried a gun, slept in the car with the stuff in his charge. There was a constant feud between the American Embassies of London and Berlin over these shipments ; they could not understand the use of a courier to bring barrels of flour and cases of tinned stuff — it upset all tradition — while we cared less for tradition than we did for our comfort. At one moment, I remember, all our correspondence from Washington, as well as our personal letters, reeked of whisky ; a bottle had smashed in transit, and our offices gave out a dissipated odor during the week.

I was given the passport bureau in the Chancery. It was a very different task from the one I had had in London at the outbreak of the war. Now we were scrutinizing the applicants with the most painstaking care, going into their documents, antecedents, investment of funds. The most difficult cases, of course, were men of military age with double nationality. It was extraordinary the number of young men in Germany who had claim to American nationality either because they were born there of German parentage, or because they were born in Germany of parents who had previously been naturalized in the United States. It would probably never have occurred to the vast majority of them to claim American citizenship had they or their parents not seen the possibility of escaping the obligations of military service, or had the war not broken out. The interviews were often heart-rending since a refusal meant that youths would be torn from their families and sent to the front. By that time there was no further illusion about war so that all realized the strong probability that departure for the front meant departure for all time. Mothers would break down and lead the boys off sobbing, fathers would tell me that starvation would face the family if the only bread-winner were taken off. And the worst of it was that the law itself was so unclear. There were so many doubtful cases that it tore you to ribbons to deal with them. Some would try to buy their immunity and offer what they had for the certificate of citizenship that meant so much more than gold to them. Some of these cases were easier to handle.   You could work yourself into indignation at the thought that they had dared to offer a bribe ; but even that was hard to do.   The thing meant so terribly much to them, and they were so often offering sums that I knew meant destitution to them.   One offer, happily, I could laugh at ; an American jockey came in who had been riding for one of the big stables.   His case was clear.   He had every right to a pass-port.   He was a native-born citizen who had been simply too careless to keep his papers in order and he had every docu-ment to prove it.   I issued him a passport.   He thanked me and said, 'Here, you have been very decent to fix me up, buy yourself something to remember me by.'   Whereupon he handed me a hundred dollar bill in American currency.   When I handed it back he was hurt and puzzled.   He said, 'But I have had a grand season, and I want another American to be glad with me.'   I compromised and said he could buy me a drink. We adjourned to the Adlon bar, and I learned more about life on the turf than a layman really ought to know.

It was difficult indeed to construct a questionnaire that would cover the variety of cases presented to us, but after many exhaustive examinations, I was able to narrow the in-quiry somewhat and to concentrate on two principal ques-tions, namely — where was the applicant educated between the years of fourteen and twenty, and where did the applicant have his money invested.   If the answer to the two questions was in the same sense, it was fairly safe to assume that the appli-cant's sympathies lay in that direction ; the reassurance lay in the coincidence of his sentimental preference with his material interest.   If a man had received his education in the United States and his money was invested there, it was a reasonable assumption that he was a loyal citizen.   If, on the contrary, his education or his investments were alien, the case needed further investigation as he might be torn by divided loyalty.   Education during this impressionable age was the factor of the highest importance.   So deeply was this borne in on me that subsequently I have unfailingly urged Americans living abroad to send their children to the United States for their education, otherwise the children feel without roots and as if they never really belonged to a particular country.   There are countless unhappy examples of American youths kept abroad by their parents during the years of education.   These young men always arouse my sympathy as they are seldom happy either when they return to the United States or when they reside abroad, they belong neither to one country nor to the other.

The Ambassador had deep interest in my passport office. His years of service in Berlin had given him a wide acquaintance among the dubious cases, and he took vigorous and prompt decision when consulted.   I got in the habit of going to his office once a day with a bundle of doubtful cases under my arm on which I had written tentatively my own recommendations.   On one application I had written 'favorably recommended' since the man's papers were entirely in order, and I had no personal knowledge of him.   The Ambassador seized a large red pencil, drew heavy lines through my recommendation, and wrote, 'This blighter' (only he did not say 'blighter') 'is the head of the League of Truth.   Refused.'

Passports make me think of the good old times, lots of things do, as you will have seen.   I made a trip around the world more than thirty years ago and carried a passport with me as I had been advised that there were certain countries in the world, notably Turkey and Russia, where it was essential to have them.   I put the passport in the bottom of my trunk ; months later on arrival at Constantinople, I looked for it under the eye of an Inspector but could not find it.   With this proof of my bona fides, the Inspector seemed content, and I went ashore with the others.   Now when you travel in Europe you cannot proceed more than a drive and a mashie shot without crossing a frontier ; not only is a passport necessary, but a whole series of different colored visas, sometimes a sworn declaration showing the various currencies in your possession. A lot of evil things began with the war, not the least vexatious of them is the institution of the passport system.

My days were filled with active work.   I would reach the office at ten, working from then until half past six or seven, with frequent continuation into the evening.   Before going to the office I would have put in an hour and a half on German — half an hour of preparation and one hour lesson.   Sunday morning most of us turned up at the Chancery to talk over the events of the week, read the telegrams and try to keep abreast of the political developments.   The Ambassador and Joe Grew would often join us and tell of their conversations, their hopes and fears.   It was a happy Chancery because we were all made to feel that we had a part in the real developments and were encouraged to think and offer suggestions on them.

These months were of the greatest educational value ; it was as if a curtain had been rolled back from a world of which I suspected the existence, but where I had never before entered.   I began to appraise motives and influences, I began to realize why political steps were taken, I began to note the effect of changing popular opinion upon policy, as well as the rise and fall of influences, personal and other and the resultant policy which in certain cases could be definitely predicted. We followed with breathless interest the struggle for power that was going on in Germany, we debated the eventual predominance of Falkenhayn or the Hydra, the palace crowd about the Kaiser, or the High Command on the Eastern Front, and tried to foretell what the success of each might mean to military questions, to the possibility of negotiation. We watched the fluctuation of opinion in our own country, and its effect upon the continuous flood of notes, protests, and instructions. Much of it was hidden, most of it was guess-work, but we followed passionately any rumor, any straw that might show which way the wind would blow. I had the benefit of the views of men of much wider experience than myself in this part of the world, and gained an insight into policy, problems, and personalities which stood me in good stead when later I had to do reporting from Switzerland on the whole scope of Central European activity.

CHAPTER XIII

Even in the sunshine and the foliage of the summer, Berlin presented an appearance that was shabby and drab. The houses needed painting, the streets were unswept for that usually immaculate city ; the people were neatly dressed, but their clothes were threadbare and carefully patched. Little traffic moved on the streets, a few cabs with worn-out horses, the motor of a foreign diplomat or of the military authorities and an occasional ancient taxi sputtering and coughing out black fumes. Gasoline was only on sale for certain licensed vehicles, and what was available was a substitute made from coal. You set out for real adventure when you took a taxi in those days. One snowy night just before Christmas I summoned one to take me to my house on the Lutzow Ufer. The taxi complained all the way, and when we reached the bridge over the canal it sighed and halted. I started to get out and the whole bottom of the car dropped into the snow, leaving me standing upright inside.

The population was apathetic. Victory had gleamed so often before them, but always decisive victory had slipped away and faded into the dull misery of trench warfare. Even the invasion of Rumania roused little enthusiasm : few people persuaded themselves that this meant a decision in the war. They had suffered losses in their families, destruction of their businesses, repeated disappointment in the early promise of victory, and always increasing fear of starvation. The rich

187

could still buy meagre quantities of food by illicit means ; in spite of the stringency of the regulations and the severity of punishment for their infraction, a considerable business of illegal dealing called 'schleichhandel' still went on.   The poor had no such resource, they had to be content with allotments of food permitted under government regulation ; it was just, but only just, sufficient to keep body and soul together and consisted mostly of heavy bread and rations of turnips.

The obtaining of rations was accompanied by unbelievable vexation.   Near our house was a station for the issue of milk. Only those could obtain this luxury who had little children or whose doctors, under strict supervision, had certified to its medical necessity.   Twice a day the line would gather in the snow or rain, hours in advance of the moment of the opening of the bureau, women and children holding their little jugs, waiting in patience.   The office would open, the issue would continue sometimes twenty minutes, sometimes half an hour, the office would close, the supply exhausted.   A third of the crowd would turn away, their chance of milk gone for that day.   All food stuffs were issued on the presentation of tickets, but the fact that you had a ticket, however restricted the amount it called for, did not at all assure you of getting the food.   That depended on the amount the shop had in stock, and it was seldom enough for all comers.   A shabby little man came to my house each morning to give me my German lesson.   Once I got up late and was having my coffee when he came in ; his nostrils literally quivered when he caught the smell, so I offered him a cup.   He took three, then apologized and told me that that was the first coffee he had had in four- teen months ; he remembered the exact date of his last taste,

that the government issued him a ration for some sort of substitute made of unmentionable substances, but that he could
not drink it and had been breakfasting on a piece of bread and
a glass of hot water. He suggested that I reduce his pay and
give him coffee each morning.

They have marvelous qualities of patience and endurance. I
conceived then and still hold the greatest respect for the German people. Their civilian population tolerated conditions that
would have driven any other of the western races to revolution,
of that I am sure. Later in the war I travelled a good deal in Allied countries and nowhere did I find the civilian population living under similar conditions of strain. After America entered
the war, my sister sent me a menu from a New York hotel, in order to show me the war restrictions that the people of the United
States were voluntarily assuming. A notice on the menu urged
the patrons of the hotel to economize on those things capable of
being shipped to France for the troops, especially articles containing white flour, and to confine their orders as far as possible
to lobsters, soft shell crabs, oysters and other sea food, as well
as corn bread, corn muffins, etc. It was a diet that even in
Switzerland made my mouth water, and as for the German on
his diet of turnips, it would have been Heaven. Whereas in
most fighting countries the people at home sent packages of
food to the soldiers at the front, in Germany it was the soldiers
with their relatively better rations who carried packages of
food as presents to their families when they went home on
leave.

At times I would hear the blare of a trumpet, and the sound
of singing coming through the window of my office. I would
lean out and watch a band of recruits come down the Wil

helmstrasse. They were mostly boys so young that it brought a lump to your throat. They had little bunches of flowers thrust into the muzzles of their rifles and sang as they marched along or laughed and joked with one another. But accompanying them was a little group of tragic-faced women, not joking, not singing, looking at their boys. There is nothing in life more touching than the swagger of a child before the unknown nor than the mute tragedy of the parents unable for the first time to share the child's experience and take over some of his suffering, aware from their own experience of what he will have to face. Many of the boys were 'freiwillige,' volunteers, who had hurried into man's estate and suffering before the law made it obligatory. I used to feel that I could distinguish the volunteers from the drafted by their very manner of marching. I do not know which was the more touching.

The poignancy of the memory of the departure of these boys for the front brings to my mind the question which has haunted my generation for almost twenty years : what can nations do to prevent a repetition of the war ? In practically all nations since the war, and especially among the democracies, this question has been of burning interest and many different attempts have been made to find the way which will render war if not impossible, at least improbable. I have no intention of dealing with the official efforts. I have been too closely associated with many of them for years to make it seemly that I should treat of them in this narrative form. What comes to my mind now is the spontaneous and popular effort arising from the determination of the peoples themselves to prevent a recurrence of the tragedy in our generation.

Peace societies are widespread, and an enormous amount of energy, enthusiasm, and money have been poured out in propaganda against war. In general this propaganda tends to build up a repugnance for war by an exposure of its horrors and miseries. Travelling in the United States I have encountered young men who have told me that under no consideration would they bear arms for their country. Occasional references are published in the press to anti-war resolutions in our Universities. With the motives which inspire most of these activities I have the fullest sympathy. But it seems to me that what the peace societies are doing is preaching to those who are already converted. I have yet to encounter a mature, responsible man or woman who does not already feel a deep repugnance to war. No one wants to fight, provided he can get what he wants without fighting, but at some point, I submit, all nations will fight and no propaganda will stop them if the cause seems sufficient. There seems to me no doubt that any nation will resist invasion of its territory. Between that point and wars of pure aggression and conquest lies that whole range of debatable territory known as 'national necessity,' 'vital interests' and 'national honor.'

The thought of a deliberate war of aggression against the United States seems wildly improbable. Our area and resources are so vast, the distance of our shores from any possible enemy strong enough to make the assault a reality, is so great that an attack could only conceivably be carried out by an enemy of vastly greater naval power than ourselves, and at such risks to himself that in comparison it makes Napoleon's attack on Moscow seem like betting on a certainty. I am excluding from this argument the problem of the Philippines.

From geographical and strategical consideration, an aggression of the islands might come within the bounds of possibility, and I am excluding it both because the law of 1934 granting the Philippines independence provides that the President may negotiate a special status for the islands and because our future relationship to them is still undefined and will presumably be so for a few years more. Especially I am excluding it because their relationship complicates the clarity of the picture, and my argument becomes simpler if we can assume for the moment that the law has gone into effect, and that the Philippines are, in legal phraseology, 'alien territory.' I take it, then, that we can rule out of our calculations, for the sake of argument, the possibility that we will be faced with the threat of war arising from the necessity of preserving our native soil against willful aggression. There remains the debatable territory of which I spoke above ; at what point will 'national necessity, vital interest or national honor' bring about a condition in the opinion of our public where war becomes not only 'inevitable' but a 'sacred cause' ?

That point will be reached the sooner or the later, according to the education or lack of it of our people. If we as a people are thoroughly informed on the international questions which may bring us into trouble, then indeed it will be hard to bring us into a war ; if we are uninformed it will be so much the easier. If we can think out in advance those causes which we consider worth fighting about we will not run the risk of being carried off our feet by a wave of war hysteria arising over an incident which we had discarded in our calmer moments as an insufficient reason for war. Let us put it more positively ; let us think out in advance, and under normally peaceful conditions, those things that we do not consider sufficient reason for war, let us be perfectly clear in our mind what they are. The danger lies in not knowing exactly what the people want now and will want in the final analysis ; the government, in the lack of such knowledge, must do its best to protect our interests at all points and so runs the risk of getting the nation into a position where there is no retreat without humiliation, and 'national honor' is involved. If it could know in advance that the point in question was one which would not be fought for, the government would never place itself in such a position.

We ought to clear up in our minds one question, not the only question by any means, but a striking one : are we or are we not, ready to fight for the maintenance of our right to trade with any and all belligerents, are we ready to forego our claim to 'neutral rights' or are we ready to fight for them ? Our present neutrality legislation clears a portion of the question, not all. I am not going to argue our position on this point. I will merely point out incidentally that our 'historical position' in respect to neutral rights is an 'historical position' for us only in periods when we were neutral and not when we were belligerent. What I should like to see is a greater measure of clarity in our national consciousness as to whether, in time of stress and economic depression and in sight of the temptation of big profits and plenty, we will decide to have our cake of peace or try to eat it too. Shall we be content with peace and resign ourselves to hard times, or shall we try to have peace with plenty and risk the peace ?

Legislation does not settle the problem, far from it. The problem will be settled by the will of the American people, and it will be settled quickly and decisively by that will in the moment of crisis. Legislation may or may not be in accord with that will ; if it is not so in accord, it will be swept quickly away. Hence I come back to the matter of education of our people. On that education will depend their decision in a moment of crisis. If they have decided for themselves what they want, they will not be swayed by the storm of propaganda that will break over our heads at the outbreak of hostilities elsewhere, they will not be influenced to the same extent by mass suggestion, they will have determined their path in calm before the event and they will have a chance of sticking to it.

The list of the questions that we ought to consider in advance could be compiled by any student. Frank Simonds in the *Price of Peace* reaches the conclusion that the only hope of peace lies in the nations of abundant resources making the necessary sacrifices and renunciations to bring about 'the assurance of economic security to the peoples of all the great powers.'

I wish that more of the enormous effort of our peace movement could be diverted to careful analysis and discussion of the dangers which might threaten our peace and to public discussion on what our attitude should be in various eventualities. The result of such discussion and public expression of opinion would be illuminating and a guide of inestimable value to the government. Every mature man and woman knows, at least vicariously, the horrors of war ; peace machinery is, I think, adequate ; it is clarity and calmness of judgment that is needed. Without such clarity and calmness, disinclination for war will not be a deterrent, and peace machinery will crash. 'In time of peace, prepare for war,' but prepare for it by careful thought as to the policies and renunciations that will be necessary to prevent it.

I have mentioned the young men in America who have told me that they would not under any consideration bear arms for their country, a statement which the great majority of people will find shocking and an evidence of cowardice. I regard it as neither the one nor the other. It is a protest of young people who believe that stupidity and worse on the part of those in charge of the government may bring them into a conflict for which they of their generation will have to pay the penalty while those responsible sit at home and preach patriotism. The young men are trying, so far as they can, to serve notice that they will not be the victims of stupidity or cupidity. They do not realize that it is they and the other mass of citizens who will have the final determination for war or peace. Nor do they realize that under the excitement of a threat of war, they may become the very ones who will clamor most loudly, if not for war, for those policies that will inevitably lead to conflict. Let us be under no misapprehension ; in the last few years, at least so far as the democracies are concerned, it has been the very people to whom war is the most profoundly repugnant, who are the most deeply convinced of the necessity for an ordered and legalized world, that have urged most insistently those policies which if pursued might have brought on a general cataclysm. Perhaps they are right, and the creation of an ordered world is worth the risk of war. This I am not discussing. I merely insist that we must urge no policy which carries with it the slightest risk, without having thought through the problem, without having reckoned the cost.

Thus I say that the attitude of these young men is not shocking, it is merely misguided. They can contribute a much greater deterrent to the possibility of the nation entering a war by a calm study of those things which may involve us, by a clear-eyed vision of the future and by public discussion and advocacy of those policies or renunciations which will keep us away from the risks of war. Their present attitude is mere futility, it is a holier-than-thou attitude towards mankind. If it could become intelligently canalized, if they could study widely and wisely and awaken public opinion to a realization of just where our dangers lie, if they could crystallize our thought as to what is worth and what is not worth a struggle, then indeed youth would have proved itself wiser than age and would have performed an incalculable service to our country.

I shall add only a word as to the conception that the position of these youths is based on cowardice. One of the best and bravest men that I knew during the war was a 'conscientious objector,' a Quaker whose faith would not let him fight. He was at the front in ambulance work for years and after the war was one of the first to organize relief for the starving children in the Central Powers while the blockade was still being maintained. In time of national enthusiasm it takes real courage to refuse to fight, probably more than to fight. The 'Conshie' has to be willing to face sneers and ostracism, if not sometimes more definite punishment. It isn't cowardice that animates these young men, it is bewilderment and irritation at a social order that has found no substitute for war. Perhaps they can find us the substitute if they will turn to positive work instead of to negative obstruction.

When I heard the singing and leaned from my window in the Wilhelmplatz to watch the boys marching by, I had no thoughts such as these in my mind. I felt the despair of the mothers, the touching braggadocio of the boys and hoped and prayed that our lads would not have to go and that my country would be spared such an ordeal as Germany was going through. I felt in myself a dull anger at the stupidity of the whole proceeding and wondered if the human mind could not find a better way to settle our affairs. I knew that history was against my hope, I knew that human beings in certain phases were against my hope. Nevertheless the hope did spring up in me ; in spite of the past twenty years of repeated failure and discouragement, that hope still abides in me. We must keep on hoping and trying ; the alternative is too appalling, the road of resignation can lead only to chaos.

With a small detour, I could make my way to the Chancery through the Tiergarten, surely one of the pleasantest of gardens in the heart of a great city. In the sunny days of early autumn I always chose this way. I used to make a circuit of the Rose Garden and offer my morning salute to Kaiserin Augusta Victoria clad in a corset of 1880 no less rigid than the grey stone from which she is carved. There is something unusually comic about contemporary figures in stone or marble, perhaps we realize subconsciously that none of us is worth perpetuating and that there is an element of irony in the futile effort of people to defeat nature's rule of 'dust to dust.' Not that the antique or so-called antique lacks comedy as well. My way led me across the Siegesallee, at that time terminating in the colossal wooden 'Hindenburg,' and a short walk between the heroes could bring cheer to the most ruffled soul.

Little children were playing in the garden, flaxen hair blowing as they ran, blue eyes laughing, shrill voices raised in anger or jubilation. Large elderly gentlemen took the air ; they carried their hats or hung them on little hooks especially prepared in their lapels, their white hair stood stiffly erect in the sun. Dachshunds pattered solemnly after them. Certain words always seem funny to me, 'dachshund' is one of them. He is one of the cleverest of creatures, and his life is one long effort to maintain his dignity and solemnity in spite of the comic body and gait the Lord gave him. The war seemed far away, sometimes you could forget it for a few minutes in these surroundings. It was a brief sight of the German people as all the world has loved them, comfortable, easy, loving the sunlight and the out-of-doors.

Immediately I reached my office and took up the day's work, the brief impression of peace evaporated. I was conscious again of living in the centre of a vast half-moon of war, broken only by Switzerland in the south. Men were dying by the tens of thousands on the Somme to gain a few yards of muddy ground, or Mackensen was rolling back the Rumanians and seizing Bucharest, or a ship was being torpedoed in the sea around the British Isles.

I have written earlier of the tales of atrocity and of the effect they made on me. On this side of the battle-line as well, not a day passed without its tale of cruelty and wanton destruction. French airplanes had flown over Karlsruhe, had singled out a school house and bombed it while classes were on, killing some forty children. Australians took no prisoners and massacred the troops in captured trenches after they had surrendered. A British ship captain had rammed a submarine after his ship had made the signal of surrender. Unspeakable horrors were perpetrated by the Russians and Rumanians on helpless prisoners. Allied airplanes repeatedly bombed hospital units plainly marked with the Red Cross, and Allied artillery shelled such units. Such were the tales which the Germans told and believed. The only tales that did not match the atrocity stories of the other side were those of horrors to the civilian population in occupied territory. Fortunately for the Germans they had no such sections of their population under enemy control. I do not recall lightly these dreadful things, or the dreadful state of mind that made them all believed readily and uncritically. I do it because it is a true representation of what went on in Germany at the time and to emphasize that nearly every war phenomenon is mutual, is felt as strongly on one side as on the other.

The German people believed passionately that they were fighting for the right. They thought that their existence was threatened by jealous enemies, they believed that Edward VII had encircled them with devilish cunning and that their enemies had seized the present opportunity to crush them. They had the same intimate conviction as most nations that they were fighting God's battle. If there were people in Germany at that time who had contrary ideas, I never came across them. It was only after we entered the war and the pressure of starvation had made itself further felt in Germany that I began to encounter Germans who believed that a responsibility lay on their Government for the outbreak of the war. Even when I returned to Berlin after the war it was rare indeed to find a German who admitted the justice of the 'war-guilt' clause of the Treaty of Versailles, and even those few claimed that other

Governments shared the same guilt. Historians will continue to debate this matter hotly, writers will try to apportion the share of responsibility resting upon each Government involved so long as men think of the Great War as contemporary or immediate history. It will only cease to interest them when our children's children care as little about the moral issue involved as we do about the rights and wrongs of the battles of the Egyptian dynasties.

The acrimonious dispute between the American and German Governments in respect to submarine warfare dragged on. It rose into acute crisis with the sinking of the *Arabic* and the *Suffolk*, only to recede to the background with renewed assurances from the German Government. Always it was present in our minds. We knew something, not much, of the struggle which went on to gain the Emperor's approval to the unrestricted use of the submarine. We knew that Von Tirpitz was advocating it strongly, that Bethmann-Hollweg on the other hand was sure that it would bring the United States into the war and was opposing it to the limit of his tired abilities. We did not know how the High Command, Hindenburg and Ludendorff, stood on the subject. It is interesting to note that recent history, based on much wider knowledge, obviously, than was available to us at the time, shows that the High Command had not taken a definite stand on the problem until immediately before the final decision was taken.

Towards the end of December, an officer attached to our Consulate General in Hamburg reported to the Ambassador that at a dinner held among a group of naval officers in that city, it became known definitely that the submarine com-

manders were shortly to put to sea carrying orders for the
prosecution of 'unrestricted' warfare. We were not sure of
this news, but it seemed to be authentic ; in any case it was
in harmony with our fears and deductions at the time. It
looked as if the end were near, for we none of us had the
slightest doubt that a declaration of 'unrestricted' submarine
warfare by the German Government would be followed by
vigorous action by the American Government, a break of relations or a declaration of war.

Several weeks dragged by and our apprehensions somewhat
diminished as no confirmation came of the report from Hamburg. But on January 31, 1917, the Chancellor made public
announcement that the German Government would wage unrestricted submarine warfare from the first of February on.
Sunday, February fourth, was a bright winter day. I walked
to the Chancery through the Tiergarten, my steps creaking on
the cold snow as I wondered how soon I would leave this
scene. As I entered the Embassy I encountered Joe Grew.
Without a word he handed me a copy of the noon paper, the
'B.Z. am Mittag.' To this day I can see that headline – how
it was printed and spaced. 'Wilson bricht die Beziehungen
mit Deutschland ab.' 'Wilson breaks off relations with Germany.'

There was no news from Washington in the Embassy ; I
remember we all sat in the Ambassador's office for a long time
for the most part in silence. Everything had been said, there
was little to add now. At length Joe and I set off and walked
slowly back through the Tiergarten. We were lunching at
my house and arrived late, so found the other guests already
seated at table. Alice Grew was there, Edith von Kleist,

Gertie von Böcklin and others. The dining room was pale blue in decoration, there were gay groups of flowers and birds painted on the walls, sunlight poured through bright chintzes. When Joe read the news from the paper the faces at the table turned white and stricken, and more than one person choked with sobs.

The next morning confirmation arrived from Washington, together with orders for the disposition of papers and codes, instructions as to where the various members of the staff and Consular Officers were to proceed.   I was ordered to the Legation at Berne, Joe to the Embassy at Vienna.   Our interests were to be handled by the Spanish Government while British interests, until that time under our charge, were to be handed over to the Legation of the Netherlands.   Strenuous days began for us all.   Not only did we have our houses to close and our personal affairs to look after, but the work of preparing the Embassy for our departure was laborious.   Jerry Gherardi, the Naval Attaché, and I made up a team for the destruction of confidential papers and cipher codes, since the German Government had told us that no more ciphered messages could be received or sent.   We worked in the cellar, piling stuff into the furnace, stripped to the waist, dripping with sweat and covered with coal dust.   I would never have believed that destruction was so laborious, papers and books do not burn, even in a hot furnace, if you throw them in in bulk.   You have to tear out leaves and crumple them almost individually before they will burn properly.   I tore paper until my hands bled, while Jerry acted as stoker, wielding a huge iron poker to stir the mess and make it burn.   We looked like the engineer and fireman in a locomotive cab on a hot night.   At last it was

all done to our satisfaction so we washed, had a drink and reported to the Ambassador that all confidential papers and codes
were destroyed.   At that moment the code clerk announced
that a short message in cipher signed 'Bryan' had just been delivered by ordinary messenger from the telegraph office.   We
were all aghast.   Codes gone, there was no possible way to find
what the message was about.   It might be of the utmost importance and indicate a complete change of policy on the part
of the American Government.   There was nothing to do,
we had to carry on as if we had not received it and trust to luck.
When I reached Berne, I deciphered the message ; it read, 'Report the whereabouts and welfare of Jacob Rabinovitch son
of American citizen now residing Berlin advise cost of cable —
Bryan.'   How that belated message ever trickled through I
have never learned.

In arranging our personal affairs we had all been somewhat
apprehensive about letting our wives go out of the house to
visit the shops, instruct the packers, or even to visit their friends
and say good-bye.   We feared the public feeling might turn
high and that they might meet with unpleasant incidents.   We
need not have worried ; we found among the Germans either
apathy or despair.   In spite of the declarations of the naval
authorities that the submarines would prevent the arrival of a
single American soldier in France, well-informed people were
crushed at the thought that a power of such inexhaustible resources had been added to the ranks of the enemy.   The man
on the street did not seem to care, the whole world was against
Germany, what did it matter to have one more enemy ?   So
there were no incidents, we and our wives did such business
as was necessary in an entirely normal way.   The gloom and

fatigue of Berlin merely deepened, another call on their almost inexhaustible patience, a further ground for discouragement, again the flicker of a hope for peace had been extinguished and the end of the war infinitely removed.

In retrospect, the most extraordinary factor of this period was its lack of drama. Here was a decision reached by the German Government, in full knowledge of its gravity, that meant the adoption of a weapon that might bring their adversaries to their knees in a brief period. On the other hand, it meant also the entry into the ranks of the enemy of an adversary of immense potentiality, wealth, and man power. If the weapon failed to be effective within a few months, the might of America would make itself felt, and the Germans were almost certainly beaten. It was a gamble, probably one of the most gigantic gambles in history. They staked on one throw, not only the fate of their nation, but the whole future of Europe. One might have expected excitement, passionate discussion, even violence. Nothing of the sort. Berlin did not look in the least different, no crowds gathered around the bulletins, no demonstrations occurred, no enthusiasm was evoked or excitement apparent. The mighty drama was played in the minds of a few men. The clash of their wills, their reckoning of the cost, their decision for the terrifying throw of the dice took place in quiet discussion in the German Great Headquarters at Aachen. Berlin, the capital, every one of whose millions was deeply affected, remained apathetic. The contrast between the patient quiet of the population and the magnitude of what was happening was the only drama.

We were busy working things out with our successors.

Fiscovitch and Rolland, Counselor and Secretary respectively
of the Spanish Embassy, were in our offices continually, learning to understand the organization, filing system, and questions
that would continue to be handled after our departure. The
Counselor of the Legation of the Netherlands, Rappard,
afterwards Minister to Berne and my good friend, was doing
the same work for the British interests and familiarizing himself with what he would have to carry on. We spent one entire day with Fiscovitch and Rappard, putting the seals of the
American and Spanish, or the American and Dutch Embassies
on all sorts of cupboards and safes that they would not need
in their work. I found some of these seals intact when I came
back, a little more than three years later, little red blobs of
wax with the seals of the Embassy fixing a linen card with my
name and Rappard's written on it.

We were notified that the special train which would take us
direct from Berlin to Zurich would pull out of the station late
in the afternoon of February 10. There was a clamor for
places on board. The staff of the Embassy was to go, of
course ; there was very little extra space, this we allotted prin-
cipally to American women who wanted to leave the country
with us. Also we took a number of newspaper men, although
the majority of them did not leave the country until the United
States actually declared war. Some of them even remained
beyond that time. Von Wiegand, for instance, was interned,
but it was internment de luxe as he was merely confined to the
Adlon Hotel until his departure could be arranged. Guido
Enderis, at that time Associated Press correspondent, under
orders from his organization, remained in Germany for the

duration of the war. He was in no way molested, although his opportunities for sending news were practically non-existent.

A company of soldiers guarded the entrance to the station and held an entire platform vacant for us, but it was unnecessary, no one paid much attention. A few accidental passers-by looked at us curiously but without hostility or indeed without any evidence of deep interest. The platform itself was practically deserted. Adolf von Montgelas dressed in black represented the Foreign Office. He had been well known to all of us through his American wife and his having handled American affairs in the Foreign Office. We realized that our departure was a great disappointment to him, he had done his utmost to prevent the rupture and had shown real courage in his persistent opposition to the unrestricted use of the submarine. A handful of friends were there besides and an officer who had been detailed to escort the Ambassador to the frontier.

We gave up the sleeping accommodations to the women and sat up all night. My wife had foreseen this probability and had packed and brought on board a luncheon basket of food and wine of Pickwickian dimensions. We demolished the basket and played cards until dawn broke as we crossed the Rhine, ran through Schaffhausen and so along into Zurich. We poured out of the train and rushed to the station shop. There was chocolate for sale, and ham sandwiches, and real coffee, no card to be presented and no line of patient half-nourished people waiting their turn. We were suddenly joyous, even hilarious ; we felt as though we had just been released from school for a holiday. The people standing by grinned and waved at us, pleased with our evident enthusiasm. I don't think any of us realized until that moment of release the tension at which we had been living, and the fatigue which suddenly came over us came as a real surprise. We boarded another train and slept all the way to Berne.

CHAPTER XIV

The Bellevue Palace Hotel at Berne was like one of the more lurid chapters in a novel of international adventure. Representatives of all races were there as was the General Staff of the Swiss Army which had been mobilized at the outbreak of the war and was not disbanded until after the armistice. Enemies bumped into one another in the elevator, found themselves at the same desk talking to the conciérge, ate in the same dining room. Frequently the enemies had been acquaintances or even friends in past years ; now they looked through each other at meeting and did their best to pretend the other was nonexistent. The dining room itself had hard and fast zones, for all that the boundaries were invisible. At one end sat the Germans, Austro-Hungarians, Turks and others of the Central Powers, at the other end the Allies had their tables. In between was a kind of no-man's-land of neutrals. There had sat the Americans until, after our breach of relations with Germany, the head-waiter had solemnly moved us into the Allied zone. Unfortunately, as the latest comers, we had to take a table at one end of a sort of whispering gallery. In the diagonal opposite corner of the room the occupants of another table, by some freak of acoustics, could hear every word said at ours, and we could profit, if we so desired, by their conversation. Since the other table was occupied by von Schubert, Bethmann-Hollweg, a nephew of the Chancellor, and other members of the staff of the German Legation, conversation at both ends of the party-line was extremely dampened.

The place was overrun with spies. To our colored imagination, most of the occupants of 'no-man's-land' who could have dealings with both sides, fell into this category. There were business men, exiles, mysterious silent gentlemen of hidden purposes. There were exotic-appearing fashionably dressed women who dined alone and maintained a rigidly correct decorum. In addition to the permanent guests at the hotel were nondescript individuals who arrived on errands or were servants employed by the guests. Once one of the Secretaries of our Legation seized an individual who was about to escape from the window of the Secretary's room to the balcony of the next room. In telling me of his capture he said that he started off with his prisoner to deliver him to the police, but as he went downstairs the thought came to him that the prisoner might be in the employ of an Allied mission and a horrid scandal would ensue, so he let him go. For everybody had spy systems to catch everybody else, including friends. Trust never extended beyond a single nationality, and even within that nationality trust was not universal. My wife had a warm friend, an American woman whom we had both known for years in Washington, who had married a German. She was expecting a child, so was my wife, so the friend came to our rooms in my absence to talk it all over, and they had a lot to discuss. My wife had not happened to mention the matter to me so I was completely taken aback a few days later to receive a note from the French Embassy warning me that my wife was engaged in intercourse with the 'enemy.' I hurriedly went down to the French Embassy to explain, convinced that if I did not remove this record, my wife would have serious difficulty the next time she attempted to cross the French frontier.

Up to this time in my life I had never encountered a spy outside of the pages of a thriller and suddenly I found myself in a society where spies and spying was one of the principal subjects of conversation. I began to look into the systems maintained by the Allied Legations. They all had what they called a 'service of counter-espionage,' apparently so called to indicate that they had been forced into this activity by the enemy's iniquitous initiative in spying. I had wide knowledge later of these organizations both in the Allied Legations and in our own. But in those first weeks I came to it, so to speak, without prejudice and perhaps with that thrill of interest that the name 'spy' stirs in us all — on paper. Quickly a skepticism began to form in my mind, a sentiment which knowledge gained later did nothing to dispel. I seriously questioned then, and still question, the real value of such work. Information that is paid for is questionable information. Your agent who takes your money is more than likely to sell himself at a slightly higher price to the enemy and to feed you false news. I am not talking now of the man who goes into enemy country and risks his life to obtain information for his country, the spy by conviction, so to speak. I am talking of the paid neutral agent who has no motive but gain for the risk he takes. The really useful information that came to us came from motives other than gain. It came from Poles, from Czechs, from Alsatians ; it came from men and women, even from children who were working for an Allied victory in order to see their country restored to independence or to the land of their choice. These people did not have to be paid, they needed no counter-espionage system to report to but came freely and willingly at their own risk for what they passionately believed to be the good of their country.

The Chancery of the Legation was on the Hirschengraben, a tiny office but adequate up to that time for its staff of the Minister, one Secretary, a Swiss chief clerk and a Swiss typist. There I presented myself the morning after my arrival and made the acquaintance of my new Chief, Mr. Pleasant Stovall, of Savannah. Although I remained in Berne only a few weeks on this assignment, I was reassigned there shortly and worked long and intimately with Mr. Stovall. Editor of a Savannah newspaper, his knowledge of Europe was naturally restricted to book learning as he had had no chance in his life for personal observation. He was a gentleman and a staunch defender of his staff. We were always in trouble of one kind or another, but we could always count on Mr. Stovall's sturdy defence against an outsider. He might turn and rend us after the departure of the stranger, but that was his prerogative. I remember him best, dressed in a black cutaway, his face round and pink with a tiny white moustache, receiving his guests at the Legation with the courtesy for which his city is famous. To the end of his life he kept up his interest in his 'boys,' and from time to time I would receive from him letters in regard to what I had been doing or clippings of editorials which he had written dealing with the problems of the Foreign Service.

The city of Berne offered an agreeable contrast to the activity of the Legations and the commotion of the Bellevue Palace Hotel. It lies, that is the old town, on a high promontory of land in a bend of the river Aare. It was bright with flowers, painted statues and fountains. Its streets were tranquil ways between quaint façades over shady arcades.   The war was remote when one set foot in this old section.   The view from our windows was brilliant and theatrical, the Aare slipped below us like a moving sheet of blue glass, wooded slopes rose stiffly beyond, foothills with a background of a snow panorama of the Bernese Oberland.

If the staff of the American Legation at that time was limited, the Allied missions made up for it in numbers.   The French Embassy as well as the British and Italian Legations not only had abundant diplomatic staffs, but numerous additional groups of military officers, commercial experts for blockade questions, press and propaganda sections and others.   I made the acquaintance of a most exceptional group of men in the French press section.   They were under the command of Professor Haguenin, a professor of French literature in the Berlin University until the war.   He was a delightful conversationalist, a witty story-teller, a man who kept his sanity in war hysteria and reached the pinnacle of intellectual aloofness by viewing dispassionately a war in which his own country was fighting for existence.   He belonged to the Briand school of political thought and was haunted in the late months of the war by the fear that peace terms would be imposed on Germany that would make her resentful and threaten the future.

In culinary matters Haguenin was also outstanding.   When he invited you to lunch he met you at the door wearing an apron and hurried back to the kitchen to supervise the completion of the sauce that could only be put on the stove after the guests had arrived.   Once a number of us were discussing the best way of spending a vacation.   One loved to climb mountains, one to bathe in the Mediterranean.   When it came to Haguenin to express his opinion, he was in no doubt at all. 'I always do the same thing the month of August, and it is what I prefer in all the world. My old father lives on a farm in Normandy, and I go down to visit him. We get up late, and as soon as we meet we prepare a list of guests for the midday dinner and dispatch invitations by a boy in the old cart with its two high wheels. Then my father and I make out the menu, divide the dishes between us, tie aprons around our middles, proceed to the kitchen and get to work. About four o'clock the guests arrive, we serve them our dinner in a sort of competition, allowing the jury of guests to decide which are the best dishes.'

Two young men under Haguenin were François-Poncet and Réné Massigli, the former now French Ambassador to Berlin, the latter one of the most brilliant and competent of the permanent officials of the French Foreign Office. Massigli was hard, trenchant, with a mass of information at his finger tips. François-Poncet was an intellectual acrobat and in conversation could juggle five balls at once, each ball a different topic and all sparkling with wit and irony. These men were all former students in the Ecole Normale. It is astonishing how many of the great figures of French public life have followed courses in that school ; the word 'normalien' indicates in itself an intellectual eminence, a training of the mind which, I think, is unequalled by any other institution. Incidentally, it often indicates an intellectual aloofness coupled with an ironical view of the capacity and achievements of the rest of mankind.

The British Legation was headed by Sir Horace Rumbold. With his ruddy complexion and monocle, his solid figure and walk, he looked like a country squire. But an exceedingly sound judgment, a great capacity for work and an acute penetration of human motives gave him authority and success. He later became Ambassador in Madrid and Berlin. He had a heterogeneous collection for his assistants, Lord Acton with red beard and Germanic appearance, Lord St. Cyres, an Oxford Don and a figure from Dickens with shabby costume and impish humor. Sir Edward Naylor-Leyland, a boy scarcely out of school, sat beside Sir Horace Pynching, lean, sardonic, with the hooked nose of a bird of prey, the two stabbed at the keys of their typewriters in a sort of cellar to the little Chancery building. Orme Sargent, Robert Leslie Craigie and Savery worked above. Savery adopted Poland, became deeply interested in that country and has made his entire career there. Sargent is now a high official in the permanent staff of the Foreign Office. Sir Robert Craigie has lately been appointed Ambassador to Tokyo.

I began to study the complexities of the operation of the blockade as applied to a neutral state. The Swiss, in consultation with the Allied Powers, had organized a body known as the Société Suisse de Surveillance, commonly called the 'S.S.S.' All imports from the Allies were consigned to this organization, which undertook to see that re-exportation to the Central Powers took place only within the limits that had been prescribed in arrangements entered into between the Swiss and the Allies. There was no desire to stifle Switzerland, but at the same time there was every intention that the Central Powers should not use Switzerland as an importing medium for Allied goods. The S.S.S. involved, naturally, endless negotiation, was often extremely vexatious to the Swiss but considering the difficulties of the problem and the intensity of feeling involved worked exceedingly well.

Switzerland was in the unhappy position of lying between the hammer and the anvil from an economic point of view. They had to buy coal from Germany, the French mines were in German hands while English coal was inaccessible. At the same time they had to get wheat, copper, petroleum and other indispensable raw materials through the Allies. The result was pressure from both sides. It is to the great credit of the Swiss that they were able to withstand the pressure by balancing one against the other thus escaping subserviency to either side and maintaining a real neutrality.

There were a score of other activities in Switzerland which I set out to study in order to be prepared as far as possible for the time when we entered the war ourselves, an event which by this time I regarded as inevitable. There were the relief organizations for prisoners, the prisoners' internment camps, the work of the International Red Cross, food packages for prisoners in German prison camps only to name a few of them.

It was a great relief to be in a land of untrammeled press and to read uninspired criticism and news. In Berlin the press had shown a surprising latitude for news from the enemy side, nevertheless it was heavily censored. We got the British papers several days late via the Netherlands. We were able to compare the two reports on any event and to approximate the truth by a mean between them. In Switzerland, however, the press published news and communiqués from both sides as well as the observations of their own neutral correspondents.

Papers such as the *Basler Nachrichten* and the *Neue Zuercher Zeitung* presented, I think, more accurate pictures of the war than any which I encountered during the four years of hostilities.   William Martin in the *Journal de Geneve*, was already showing himself an authoritative critic, particularly in matters relating to the Austro-Hungarian Empire.   He was developing those qualities of careful analysis and close reasoning based on thorough documentation that made him such a power in Geneva for the first ten years of the League's existence.   It was the role of a gadfly ; William Martin stung every government in turn but usually for the general good.

I liked the Swiss at once.   I liked the order, the cleanliness, the sturdy self-respect of the nation.   This is not the time for me to write of Switzerland and the Swiss people ; I am writing only of the few weeks of my first stay there.   What I now think of that land is the result of years spent among them subsequently, of the many friends I have there, of happy years in a pleasant land among an admirable folk.   I should like some day to describe them more fully ; perhaps I shall.   Then will be the moment to testify to their common sense and moderation, to their honesty and civic spirit which has produced a government in many ways an example to the world.   I have been reading recently the memoirs of Lord Howard, who spent some time in Berne as British Minister to Switzerland.   His chapters on Berne are interesting and stimulating ; he studies the practicability of applying the Swiss system of the Federal Council to a democracy such as Great Britain and believes that much advantage could be derived from doing so.

As I have said, I was so convinced that we were about to enter the war that most of my effort through those weeks was devoted to studies preparatory to making the Legation the most effective possible instrument when we did come in. It was obvious that the present staff would be entirely inadequate for the work we would be called upon to do, so a plan of necessary personnel had to be worked out. Also the space available in the Chancery was negligible. I went about town and marked down in my own mind the necessary accommodations for the war-time activities of our own Legation. I made a tour by motor with Major Exton, the Military Attaché, of the German frontier from Basle to the Austrian border, marking down those places where offices could be established effectively for information purposes. Especially I cultivated relations with members of the Allied missions of the most varied activities, hoping to profit by their experience of more than two years of war and not have to start from scratch. They were more than ready to put their experience at our disposition, and the information that they gave me was later invaluable and enabled me to avoid innumerable mistakes and wasted effort.

A telegram came through from Joe Grew in Vienna saying that he had asked the Department of State to send me there as the staff was short handed. A few days later orders came transferring me. This was the fourth post I had occupied during one calendar year, and as I returned to Berne a few weeks later, I surely established a record by holding five posts in one year, in two of which my wife and I had been really installed in our own houses. But the period was too engrossing to think of personal convenience, the new scenes had in each case been deeply interesting. So we packed up again, but only a portion of our possessions. We left the rest at the Bellevue Palace, telling them to reserve rooms for us again in four weeks from the day. I figured that by that time the United States would be at war and we would have to leave Vienna as well. I missed the date by about three days.

The train rolled into Austrian territory at Buchs. Even in that frontier station and in the attitude of the customs officers a contrast with Germany was already apparent. The guards were friendlier, their manner was more comfortable. I decided that if I had had any treasonable matter to smuggle, I could have brought it through Buchs much easier than into Germany. We had not been long in Vienna before it became apparent that the different attitude was general and not an isolated phenomenon of the customs house at Buchs. There was the same scarcity of food, there were the same stringent regulations about food purchases, but where in Germany the authorities and a large proportion of the population were making vigorous efforts to carry out the regulations, in Vienna they seemed to exist only to be broken ; from the wealthiest man to the cab driver, everybody had some illegal means of augmenting the Government allowances. The population of Berlin was suffering intensely, they were patient and grim, but they were also determined. The population of Vienna was, I think, suffering less at that time, but they were neither patient nor grim ; they were bored with the war and were seeking any means of diversion to forget it. When you talked with them the only phases of the war that seemed to interest them profoundly were the food restrictions and their irritation at Germany. They treated us foreigners rather as confidants to whom they could pour out their troubles than as potential enemies.

The American Ambassador to Vienna, Mr. Frederick Penfield, was a curious personality. He had considerable ability, his talk and reminiscences were interesting, but his judgment was influenced by the effect that any external event would have on himself. It was as if the image of the outside world penetrated to his consciousness after having been refracted through the lens of his personality. He was unable to believe that the Austrian Government would break relations with the United States while he was Ambassador, and when the break became inevitable, he departed from the country leaving the Counselor as Chargé d'Affaires to close the Embassy and evacuate the staff. He had a large collection of medals and orders that had been given him, and some of his best reminiscence found expression when showing the collection. Mrs. Penfield was thoughtful and kindly ; she used to keep those of us who were living in hotels supplied with white bread and butter, delicacies unobtainable elsewhere. Whenever we received such a gift, my wife invariably sallied forth to purchase a return gift of flowers as some of the staff had found that obligation to the Ambassador weighed heavily, and we were unwilling to incur any.

In the Embassy at Vienna I began the close friendship and collaboration with Fred Dolbeare and Allen Dulles, both Secretaries somewhat junior to me, which lasted for years until first Dulles then Dolbeare left the service. I mean that the collaboration lasted until their departure ; the friendship still endures, and is as firmly rooted as ever.

We found Joe and Alice Grew installed in an apartment in the Hotel Bristol so we took a suite on the same floor. We had a piano sent in and in the evenings Joe would arrive and play the accompaniments while my wife sang. We never dined in the Bristol, the food was unbelievably bad.   It looked as if the hotel management were the only people in Vienna to obey the laws of food restriction.   Usually we went to Sacher's.   When I saw 'Reunion in Vienna' and Frau Sacher appeared upon the stage, I felt that I myself was on reunion. Restrictions did not seem to trouble Frau Sacher ; in any case the food was excellent.   On one unforgettable occasion Walter von Mumm was giving a party to a group of officers when we entered.   Someone had sent him a barrel of oysters from the Baltic, a nearly forgotten luxury.   He sent over to our table enormous quantities of roasted oysters, while Frau Sacher came in to enjoy the general gaiety, to be teased by the officers and to give back as good or better than she got.

The Grews had been to Vienna en poste before, so they had numerous friends among the Austrians who used to come to tea in Alice's apartment and eat enormous quantities of white bread and butter, and cakes.   Sometimes they were so numerous they spilled over into our rooms, and we had the curious sensation of entertaining people who did not know us and of whose names we ourselves were often completely ignorant. They were amusing and gay, people of the old court regime. They never obtruded their sorrows and difficulties.   They came socially and behaved as if the world were as carefree as in their youth when Paris was a day's trip away instead of being separated by an eternity.

I particularly remember a visit of Princess Daisy of Pless. She was lovely to look at and of boisterous and contagious humor.   After she had been in Alice's room a few minutes she said, as if in sudden recollection, 'Oh, I have forgotten my little man.'   She went to the door, I opened it for her and saw a shabby little middle-aged man with a drooping moustache and a derby on the back of his head. He was seated quietly on a trunk with his hands folded and looked rather like 'Mr. Milquetoast' in the cartoons. She said, 'Now I am going to be here until 7:30. It is only six now, so go off and have your supper and come back for me. I promise I won't leave until 7:30.' The little man rose, doffed his derby, bowed, and with a 'Danke, Hoheit,' shuffled down the corridor. Returning to the room, Princess Daisy explained : 'You see, I am an English woman married to a German. On both counts I am under suspicion by the Vienna police. So they have assigned a little spy to see where I go and whom I visit. At first he used to hide behind lamp-posts and try to be invisible. But I felt so sorry for him that I have now made a sort of partnership with him by which I undertake not to lose him and to tell him always how long I will stay anywhere so he can wait comfortably in a café. But remembering him is quite a responsibility.' Another and striking example of the value of the espionage system !

In spite of the brevity of my stay in Vienna, in spite of the sorrows and suffering that the people were going through, I became fond of the city and its people. They were so kindly, so friendly that it was difficult to believe that we were on the verge of entering the war against them. Even in the month of March with its foul weather, I liked to walk about the town. It has such dignity and antiquity, such ease and comfortableness. It is one of the few cities that everyone likes, and I was no exception.

The Foreign Office had warned us that the Government was under pressure from Germany to break relations with us, that they had resisted that pressure up to the moment but that if we declared war on Germany, the Austrian Government would have to sever relations and hand us our passports. We were thus warned in plenty of time and began such preparations as I have described before in the case of the Embassy at Berlin. Instructions had been issued to us individually, and I had been reassigned to Berne. I was happy about this order as I realized the extraordinary opportunity for interesting work in Berne and was eager to put into effect the measures I had already planned for the Legation. On April 10th the President declared war on Germany in a solemn and stirring declaration before Congress.

Joe Grew, Ellis Dresel and I had already left Berlin in the special train of a departing Embassy so we were able to compare our departure from Vienna with the previous one. The contrast was striking. Where in Berlin all had been grim, polite, and excessively well managed, in Vienna crowds were bustling about, and we had to struggle through to find our places. But our friends had come down to see us off, Walter von Mumm in a sky-blue German uniform arrived with his arms full of flowers for the ladies. As the train got under way, we could see handkerchiefs waved from the platform and hear the God-speeds and good luck wishes of our friends. Even the officials of the station were smiling as they stood at salute.

This story must end here. When my country entered the war, the character of my work changed abruptly. I became immediately an active participant in events and no longer merely an interested observer. People, scenes, reflections in themselves, all became shadowy and pale in contrast with the immense realities of the struggle. I cannot write of this period in the rambling and narrative form which I have used in this book. I must write it later and in another form ; a different kind of story, and of a different person.